W9-AUX-996

WITHDRAWN

THE BATTLE FOR
Beverly Hills

THE **BATTLE** FOR
Beverly Hills

A CITY'S INDEPENDENCE AND THE
BIRTH OF CELEBRITY POLITICS

NANCIE CLARE

ST. MARTIN'S PRESS ❧ NEW YORK

THE BATTLE FOR BEVERLY HILLS. Copyright © 2018 by Nancie Clare. All rights reserved. Printed in the United States of America. For information, address St. Martin's Press, 175 Fifth Avenue, New York, N.Y. 10010.

www.stmartins.com

Designed by Steven Seighman

The Library of Congress Cataloging-in-Publication Data is available upon request.

ISBN 978-1-250-12134-9 (hardcover)
ISBN 978-1-250-12135-6 (ebook)

Our books may be purchased in bulk for promotional, educational, or business use. Please contact your local bookseller or the Macmillan Corporate and Premium Sales Department at 1-800-221-7945, extension 5442, or by email at MacmillanSpecialMarkets@macmillan.com.

First Edition: March 2018

10 9 8 7 6 5 4 3 2 1

To Ed

CONTENTS

ACKNOWLEDGMENTS

Writing a nonfiction book is like taking a journey: you know the ultimate destination, but you have no idea who you will encounter or the adventures you'll have along the way. At least that is the way it was for me.

In writing this book I stand on the shoulders of giants. Everyone to whom I reached out for help or advice was beyond generous with their time and gracious in the giving of it.

My long list of people who must be thanked begins with my friend and colleague Annie Jacobsen. When I was having my moment of doubt and pain in getting this project under way, she met with me and gave me a metaphorical hit upside my head. "Of course you can do this," she said. And, as everyone who knows Annie is aware, she is always right.

Next are two people whose contributions have enriched this story beyond measure: Robert S. Anderson, great-grandson and grandson, respectively, of Margaret and Stanley Anderson, the original owners of the Beverly Hills Hotel, author of *Beverly Hills: The First Hundred Years,* who has forgotten more about Beverly Hills than most people will ever know; and Cari Beauchamp, the Mary Pickford Foundation's Resident Scholar and author of *Without Lying Down: Frances Marion and the Powerful Women of Early Hollywood.* Their respective insights into the City of Beverly Hills and Mary Pickford, the woman who drove the fight against its annexation to Los Angeles, were both illuminating and invaluable.

Authors who had written on similar subjects were instrumental as guides, saving me from going astray: John Buntin, Joel Engel, Tracey Goessel, Michael Gross, William J. Mann, Richard Rayner, and Marc Wanamaker. A special thanks to the late Kevin Starr, with whom I corresponded when the project was in its infancy and whose absence will be felt by anyone writing anything about the history of California.

Librarians are a critical resource for anyone with the temerity to write a book. I am in debt to the research desk at the History and Genealogy Department of Los Angeles Central Library and, first, to Gail Stein, and then Alice Kuo, Susan Minobe, and the staff of researchers at the Historical Collection of the Beverly Hills Public Library.

Members of law enforcement were invaluable as well. Many thanks to Clark Fogg, senior forensic specialist at the Beverly Hills Police Department, and Michael A. Fratantoni, archivist at the Los Angeles County Sheriff's Department.

No writer is an island. A huge debt of gratitude is owed to those who kept me going. My daughter, Logan Clare, who also happens to be my attorney, gets a double dose of thanks (and love); her husband, Mike Weiss, also a writer, for listening—and not nodding off—when I talked about the book; Scott Waxman of Waxman Leavell, who forwarded my pitch to agent extraordinaire Rachel Vogel, now with Dunow, Carlson & Lerner Literary Agency, who would first guide me through the proposal process and then find *Battle for Beverly Hills* a home at St. Martin's Press; the editorial team at SMP, especially Emily Angell and Elizabeth Lacks, the two stunning-in-every-way editors who made this a better book, and George Witte and Sara Thwaite, who guided it through completion; Mimi Park, who navigated me through my finances; Phil Savenick and the Beverly Hills Historical Society, whose photo collection is a true window into Beverly Hills' past; and last, but certainly not least, my husband, Ed Clare, who has given me, well, everything.

THE BATTLE FOR
Beverly Hills

Introduction

———◇◇◇———

I n the two months following the proposed annexation of Beverly Hills to Los Angeles in early 1923, the sometimes heated rhetoric between those against joining the bigger city—which included some of the world's most famous faces from the new medium of the moving pictures, Mary Pickford, Douglas Fairbanks, Tom Mix, Harold Lloyd, Rudolph Valentino, Will Rogers, Conrad Nagel, and Fred Niblo—and those in favor had been a war of words. That is, until the morning of February 26, 1923, when an "Infernal Machine," as the bomb was called in the newspapers, exploded in the hands of Al Murphy, the editor of the *Beverly Hills News*, the city's weekly paper. Mr. Murphy and the publication, which he owned as well as edited, were pro-annexation, as were many of the local real estate developers, including many of the principals of the Rodeo Land & Water Company, which had created Beverly Hills at the turn of the twentieth century.

If there was one thing that could capture the immediate attention of the residents of Los Angeles it was a bomb. In L.A., especially since the 1910 bombing of the *Los Angeles Times,* explosive devices at newspapers caught everyone's attention. The attack was covered extensively in the local papers and the story was picked up by publications across the country, bringing attention to what had been a mundane political interaction between two cities at the western edge of the United States. The battle for Beverly Hills had turned ugly.

It's reasonable to assume that most of the people in the Los Angeles area who followed the news of the bombing—and some of it, especially from William Randolph Hearst's *Los Angeles Examiner,* was breathless—must have been asking themselves: Why on earth would the suggestion of joining the City of Los Angeles spark such violent outrage? Beverly Hills was remote and geographically tiny with a population of less than a thousand; it had only been incorporated as a city for nine years. Several communities across the Southern California basin—unincorporated areas as well as incorporated cities—had voted to join Los

Angeles, especially after the completion of the Los Angeles Aqueduct, the wonder of engineering completed in 1913 by William Mulholland that brought water from the eastern slope of the Sierra Nevada Mountains through the Owens Valley. What made Beverly Hills so different? And what unique set of circumstances led to its ability to resist the lure of Los Angeles and its abundant water?

Well, for one thing, Beverly Hills was the city that Mary Pickford and Douglas Fairbanks called home. In the wake of the undisputed king and queen of motion pictures moving to the small city on the western edge of Los Angeles, many other famous faces—Charlie Chaplin, Tom Mix, and Will Rogers among them—had followed. The stars had their reasons for wanting to live in Beverly Hills, some of which were obvious, like the smaller police force separate from the Los Angeles Police Department, an important distinction in the era of Prohibition. But it wasn't all about seclusion and the privacy to drink cocktails and throw the occasional orgy (although that was part of it); there were also subtler reasons such as property values and community control.

The stars' work against annexation may all seem like a bit of a lark now. And in retrospect, these eight silent screen stars, who struck poses and emoted for the hand-cranked cameras, come off as quaint. They were anything but. They were the first generation of movie stars, and the world had not known anything like them before. They wielded power not because they had been born to it or earned the money to buy it. Their power came from the connection their audience developed with them while sitting in the darkened auditoriums watching "flickers." In fact, the timing for the battle of Beverly Hills was prophetic. When the Beverly Hills Eight, led by Mary Pickford, fought annexation, they were doing something that had never been done before. What they did was so successful that it became a model for generations of celebrities to intervene in political causes that caught their fancy or in which they had a vested interest. And over the decades people paid attention. It is now so much a part of the American political landscape that it's startling to realize that one hundred years ago, before the emergence of "movie stars," this cause-and-candidate promotion by celebrities did not exist. And whether or not they realized the long-term consequences of using their high profiles to influence an election's outcome, it dawned on the celebrities who fought the battle for Beverly Hills against the land developers and realtors that there was a shift in how they were perceived and the influence they could bring. And they were going to capitalize on it.

How and why did their campaign work? The changing times were a factor. The Roaring Twenties was an era of unprecedented turmoil, both cultural and political. On the one hand, women had finally been given the right to vote; on the other, the Volstead Act, prohibiting the consumption of alcoholic beverages, had passed. Immigrants were pouring into the country; the inexorable population shift from rural to urban that had started before the turn of the twentieth century was accelerating. As the robber barons who had capitalized on the country's growing economy after the Civil War began to lose their iron hold on commerce, and a new generation of business tycoons emerged, the stifling propriety that had gripped social conventions also began to give way.

In the two decades leading up to the Roaring Twenties, political upheaval had raged across the globe. The old order had been wrenched, often by extremely violent means, so as to be unrecognizable. The War to End All Wars, as World War One was called, had changed the face of Europe. On Europe's eastern edge, the Russian Revolution had sent shock waves through every democratic government in the world; on the western side of Europe, the Republic of Ireland had emerged from the bombs, bullets, and blood of the Irish Revolution, splitting the island and thwarting the English who had controlled the whole of Ireland for almost a thousand years. For the United States, World War One had thrown it, especially the soldiers who had traveled to Europe, into the world. There was no going back.

The profound technological disruptions of the first two decades of the twentieth century were certainly part of the equation. Telegraphy was giving way to telephony. Radio was beginning to bring news, sports, and music into homes. Gramophones were changing how the world experienced music. But it was perhaps the new motion picture industry, which had chosen Southern California as its center of operation, that had the most profound cultural impact. Motion pictures had done nothing less than change the very nature of entertainment, something that makes humans human, something that before film had always had to occur live and in real time. When the new medium was getting started in and around New York City in the earliest days of the twentieth century, no one could have predicted that the uncredited actors and actresses who appeared in the flickers would rise to such prominence and influence so quickly; that an entire industry of fan magazines would spring up and that the general population would be in thrall to the men and women whose images were projected on screens across the country. The nation simply could not get enough of these shiny new stars, and their adulation fueled a new industry.

And it was, after all, California. As much as the new residents pouring into the state might strive to remold California into replicas of the places they left behind in the East, Midwest, and South, it had always been different. For one thing, California had actually been part of Mexico in living memory, albeit those remembering would have been quite old. Reminders of the state's Spanish and Mexican past were everywhere, including the sweeping land grants that had been awarded to the Californios, as the citizens of the Spanish and Mexican colony had been called. Beverly Hills had been one such land grant, and its borders today are almost exactly those of Rancho Rodeo de las Aguas, or the Ranch of the Gathering of the Waters, awarded to the Valdez family for its support during Mexico's war of independence from Spain. The widow of the soldier to whom Rancho Rodeo de las Aguas had been granted sold the property only after defending her home in a daylong battle against Native Americans. It's not too great a flight of fancy to say that a fighting spirit was part and parcel of Beverly Hills.

Although they couldn't know it at the time, the celebrities who took a stand against annexation not only won that battle, they quite possibly changed politics in the United States—and perhaps the world—forever. In their fight against annexation by the City of Los Angeles, and probably without realizing it, they laid the groundwork for celebrity influence that is still a work in progress. In the decades that followed, actors would capitalize on the instant recognition their fame provided to champion causes and win elections to offices at all levels of government. For the most part, their fame enabled actors and celebrities to skip to the head of the line and run for higher office without working their way up the political ladder, making the necessary connections, learning the political ropes and campaigning as they moved from local to regional to state and, ultimately, national office. Among the elected offices that have been held by those who made the leap from stage and screen are city council member (Sheila Kuehl), mayor (Clint Eastwood, Jerry Springer), congressperson (Helen Gahagan Douglas, Sonny Bono), senator (George Murphy, Al Franken), governor (Ronald Reagan, Arnold Schwarzenegger, Jesse Ventura), and president (Ronald Reagan, Donald Trump).

Oddly, in a city as self-absorbed with its own legend as it is, Beverly Hills' close brush with oblivion isn't an oft-told tale. Most residents have no idea that if it wasn't for Mary Pickford and the rest of the Beverly

Hills Eight—Douglas Fairbanks, Harold Lloyd, Tom Mix, Fred Niblo, Conrad Nagel, Will Rogers, and Rudolph Valentino—at the very most their city would be a named neighborhood in Los Angeles like Hancock Park or Bel Air, instead of its own municipality. However, the spirit that drove Beverly Hills to turn down a marriage with Los Angeles is still very much alive. Beverly Hills is its own city and one to be reckoned with. It has its own laws, police force, fire department, school district, trash collection, and parks and recreation department. There are no hospitals or cemeteries in Beverly Hills, population density is low when compared with the surrounding city of Los Angeles, and high-rise buildings are almost nonexistent. Up until very recently none of the region's Metropolitan Transit Authority's stabs at mass transit—such as the subway or light rail lines—have made it inside the city's borders, although its bus routes do bisect the city. (The expansion of the MTA's "Purple Line" is slated to have two stops in Beverly Hills.) And there are no freeways running through the city. In an urban region that is sutured together by freeways, there isn't one that will take you into or out of Beverly Hills. When the freeways were being built to tie the far-flung cities in every corner of the greater Los Angeles area together, Beverly Hills said "no thanks." As a separate city, that was its right. The population of Los Angeles, about 3.9 million, might dwarf Beverly Hills' 34,700 or so residents, but in civic matters the smaller city isn't afraid to go toe to toe with its large neighbor. Beverly Hills is an independent city in every meaning of the word.

The only nod to the stars' contribution to an independent Beverly Hills is *Celluloid*, a peculiar twenty-plus-foot-tall bronze-and-marble obelisk by sculptor Merrell Gage, whose plinth features a bas-relief representation of each of the eight stars in one of their signature roles. Extending up from the squat base is a tall, narrow lance-like object around which a spool of film is unfurling. The memorial is located on a traffic island roughly the shape of a triangle at the obtusely angled intersection of Olympic Boulevard and South Beverly Drive, or South Bev as it's known, a busy intersection in one of the most, by some accounts *the* most, traffic-intensive urban area in the United States. Since the monument's installation in 1959, undoubtedly millions have driven by. Far from being the hoped-for tourist attraction, because of its inaccessibility very few pedestrians have ventured across the busy lanes of traffic to discover the remarkable event this monument commemorates. It's just there. If you're looking at it, that means you are stopped at a light or stuck in traffic. It will be in the rearview mirror before long, or so drivers hope.

Saving Beverly Hills from annexation may be what the monument on Olympic Boulevard commemorates, but it is far from the only thing the campaign accomplished. Today, listening to a celebrity advocating a cause, endorsing a candidate, or even declaring his or her candidacy for office doesn't raise an eyebrow. In 1923, when eight stars battled to keep their city free from the clutches of what they perceived as a rapacious Los Angeles, it was something new. This is the story of how the stars and the city aligned to make this come to pass.

1

Rancho Rodeo de las Aguas and the Invention of Beverly Hills

————◇◇◇————

The Beverly Hills where Douglas Fairbanks bought his first house in 1919—a hunting lodge that lacked water and electricity where he could have his secret assignations with Mary Pickford—was not too far removed from the days when the area was the Rancho Rodeo de las Aguas. Although the land Beverly Hills occupies had been part of the vast stretch of western North America claimed by Spain in the early sixteenth century, it wasn't until 1769 that an official exploration party, led by Gaspar de Portola on behalf of the king of Spain, traveled there. It's with the Rancho Rodeo de las Aguas land grant, awarded to Vicente Valdez for his service to Mexico in its war of independence against Spain, that the history of Beverly Hills really begins.

Present-day Californians tend to view the Rancho Period—the time between Mexican Independence from Spain in 1822 and California's admission to the United States in 1850—with a romanticized nostalgia. The reality of California's Rancho Period, however, was certainly much harsher for its denizens. They were probably not, as Pierce Benedict, scion of one of the city's founding families, wrote in his 1934 history, "a people prosperous and carefree, browned by the bland sunshine with nothing more urgent than watching the clouds shift patterns,"[1] or what present-day festivals around the state celebrate as a time of endless barbecues, dances, and mariachi music. In fact, considering Mexico's enormous political instability at the time, the California Rancho Period of Alta California didn't stand a chance of sustained existence. The wheels had started to come off the bus of Mexico's expanded country almost immediately after its independence from Spain. First Texas broke away, was briefly an independent republic recognized by the United States, France, and England, and then, in 1845, subsequently joined the United States. Even before gold was discovered in 1848, Alta California was in play as well. The United States made the first move on Mexican California in 1845, when the U.S.-commissioned explorer John C. Frémont and a group of armed men under his command assisted in the "Bear Flag Revolt" in Sonoma, helping local U.S. immigrants in Alta California take the same tack Texas had by declaring California a republic. Pretty much all that is left of that endeavor is the state flag, which features a California grizzly bear and the words "California Republic."

What the actions of Texas and Alta California in the 1840s made clear, though, was that Mexico in the post–New Spain era was wobbly. With pressure coming from Texas in the east and California to the north, it was only a matter of time before Mexico really started to break apart. And that time came in 1846 with the outbreak of the Mexican-American War. When the war ended in 1848, Mexico had lost about half of its territory, including what is now the state of California as well as New Mexico, Utah, Nevada, Arizona, and western Colorado. So much of history is timing, and although the Mexican-American War was the first military action in which the United States utilized the new technology of the telegraph, with news from the front arriving within days and sometimes hours of events,[2] communication in the mountains of California still depended on men traveling to cities and towns by horse or on foot. The ramifications of this disconnect could not be more profound in terms of what Mexico gave up to put a stop to the war. The Treaty of Guadalupe Hidalgo, which ended the Mexican-American War and defined the new border between the United States and Mexico in the region of California as a straight line from the mouth of Gila River to one marine mile south of the port of San Diego, was signed on February 2, 1848, in Mexico City. Nine days earlier, on January 24, 1848, James Marshall had discovered gold at Sutter's Mill in California's Sierra Nevada Mountains—a discovery that would not be reported in any newspaper until late in March of the same year.

With the dual benefits of a port on the Pacific and gold in the mountains, there was no "territory status" interregnum for California after the end of the Mexican-American War. By 1850 statehood was signed, sealed, and delivered. (By contrast, California's neighbor Arizona remained a territory and would not become a state until 1912.)

Some of Spain's common practices had carried over after Mexican independence, though, including granting huge swaths of land to friends, relatives, and political allies in Alta California. That included Sergeant Vicente Villa, who had fought for Mexico in its war of independence from Spain. Villa, who had come to El Pueblo de Nuestra Señora la Reina de los Ángeles (the Town of Our Lady the Queen of the Angels) as a six-year-old boy, eventually married Maria Rita Valdez, the daughter of Sebastiana and Eugenio Valdez, who had come to Los Angeles in about 1771, in one of the earliest group of emigrants from Mexico to Los Angeles. By most reports, Maria Valdez and Vicente Villa were married in 1808. As for how in the late 1830s Rancho Rodeo de las Aguas wended its way to Señora Valdez Villa, in the original typewritten draft of an article published in *Holiday* magazine in October 1952, Irving Stone wrote: "Sergeant Villa was given the Rancho Rodeo de las Aguas as a pension when he was invalided out of the army."[3] Upon his death in the 1830s, the land eventually became Maria Valdez Villa's.

The procedure to secure the title to a land grant was straightforward, but also cumbersome and time-consuming; it could take several years to complete the process. A parcel of uninhabited land was identified and a petition accompanied by a rude map was submitted. Once he received it, the governor of Alta California—in the case of Rancho Rodeo de las Aguas it was Juan Bautista Alvarado—would send the petition to the local *alcalde*, the municipal magistrate, who investigated the individuals involved and checked records to make sure there were no previous claims on the same parcel. Once the *alcalde* signed off, the governor made the grant. Considering the precision with which land is surveyed now, the process of determining exact boundaries and recording acreage was shockingly casual. The boundaries of the property were drawn by sighting natural landmarks that the *alcalde*, accompanied by two witnesses, confirmed by riding the borders of the land and measuring it with a riata, a woven leather rope, fifty *varas* in length. (A *vara* is approximately one meter in length.) Estimates were rough, *poco más o menos*, "a little more or less."

The exact year title to the Rancho Rodeo de las Aguas became Sergeant Villa's is even fuzzier than its original borders. Maria Valdez Villa testified the grant date was 1838, but according to the official record, Governor Alvarado granted the land to the former soldier in 1831. However, it's quite possible the written date is in error because Juan Bautista Alvarado didn't become Alta California's governor until 1836.

In Articles VIII and IX of the Treaty of Guadalupe Hidalgo,[4] the United States indicated it would confer United States citizenship to those living in Alta California and honor the land grants that had been awarded by Mexico. So even though the land was now in a different country, Maria Valdez Villa remained the owner of the Rancho Rodeo de las Aguas.

Regardless, for Maria Rita Valdez Villa, who inherited Rancho Rodeo de las Aguas from her husband in the 1830s, it was a tough slog. Maria, mother of eleven children according to Stone's account, lived with her family in two adobe houses at what is now the intersection of Alpine Drive and Sunset Boulevard in Beverly Hills. When she was working at the rancho, she ran cattle and horses and did her best to cultivate crops. But while the rancho got its name, which translates to "gathering of the waters," from the intersection of two underground streams that coursed under Cañada de las Aguas Frias (Coldwater Canyon) and Cañada de los Encinos (Canyon of the Oaks, which is now Benedict Canyon) and joined approximately where the Beverly Hills Hotel is now situated, the water's abundance could be capricious. Crops and herds would wax and wane depending on whether or not water flowed. Even though there wasn't a critical mass of people whose lives depended on the water—Los Angeles' first census, in 1836, counted less than thirty residents on the Ranch of the Gathering of the Waters—lack of a consistent water source made ranching as a profitable endeavor difficult. Maria Valdez Villa didn't even live on her rancho full time; she owned another home on Main Street in the pueblo of Los Angeles. And in some ways, not much has changed in L.A.: It took a full day to travel between the two residences, a distance of twelve or so miles.

Having another house in the relatively civilized Pueblo de Los Angeles would come in handy for Maria. California may have become a state, but it was still the Wild West. In 1852, with the ink on the statehood paperwork barely dry and the Gold Rush raging to the north, Native Americans ambushed Maria Rita on her rancho in a scenario that would become a staple in Westerns filmed in nearby neighborhoods some fifty years later. Accounts of the number of attackers at the ranch house differ. Some reports are specific, reporting three attackers; some accounts refer to a "band." Regardless, it was a pitched battle that lasted the better part of a day. When the ammunition for Maria's muskets began to run low, a nine-year-old boy managed to slip out of the ranch house, evade attackers, dodge bullets, and crawl for half a mile along a ditch to get help from ranchos in the neighboring town of Sherman, which is now West Hollywood. According to the original typewritten draft of an article published in *Holiday* magazine in October 1952, by Irving Stone, the ranchers came to Maria's aid and "drove the redskins northward to a walnut grove on which now stands the Beverly Hills Women's Club. There they shot and buried the Indians."[5] And according to Benedict's history, in 1869 three Native American skeletons were exhumed near the current site of the Beverly Hills Women's Club. In fact, Pierce

Benedict's father, Edison A. Benedict, kept the largest skeleton in the family home.[6]

Even though her family escaped the ordeal unharmed, Maria Valdez Villa had had enough. Not long after the attack, she obtained a copy of the land grant deed and sold the 4,539-acre Rodeo de las Aguas for $500 in cash, $500 in notes, and the promise of an additional payment of $3,000 after the full confirmation of the title by the U.S. government to Benjamin Davis Wilson (for whom Mount Wilson in the San Gabriel Mountains is named) and Major Henry Hancock, who eventually owned the land that became Hancock Park. Maria would have to wait more than two decades for that last 75 percent of what was owed her because the title wasn't confirmed by the U.S. government until 1871. Not long after becoming a partner in the rancho, Major Hancock transferred his half of the property to William Workman, who would become mayor of Los Angeles in late 1886 and serve two terms. (Because the majority of the payout took almost three decades, there was some scuttlebutt, never proven, that Wilson and Hancock had put the Native Americans up to attacking Maria Valdez in order to force her off the land. Considering the far-flung location of the parcel, its seemingly unfit-for-much condition, and the fact that Hancock almost immediately bowed out, the consensus is that this is unlikely. Yet it remains one of the city's origin myths.)

Over the next forty-plus years, subsequent owners would graze cattle and sheep, grow grain, endure devastating droughts, and drill for oil. In 1881 hoteliers Henry Hammel and Charles Denker bought the land that had been Rancho Rodeo de las Aguas from Wilson and Workman and renamed it the Hammel and Denker Ranch. They grew produce for their hotels, including lush fields of lima beans. In the late 1890s, Hammel and Denker decided to get involved in land speculation by subdividing their holdings. They called their development Morocco. No houses were ever built during the pair's stewardship.

Hammel and Denker were just too early to the party, because things were about to change. One look at photographs of turn-of-the-twentieth-century Los Angeles, with its wide-open, seemingly endless, unpopulated space, and it's easy to understand why men willing to take a business risk saw a city waiting to happen. Stretching as far as the eye could see was a blank vista just aching for roads, homes, offices, factories, stores, and the people who would drive, live, work, and shop there. And after the 1905 bond measure that would fund an aqueduct from the Owens Valley was passed by voters in the City of Los Angeles, there was the promise of seemingly unlimited water, the land was fertile and underneath it all there was oil.

For those with gumption and grit and a bit of luck, opportunity was everywhere. They found the business environment of lax-to-nonexistent government oversight at the turn of the twentieth century an ideal medium for growth. Huge strides in technology and transportation had been made in the three decades after the end of the Civil War. There was a transcontinental railway, first telegraph and then telephone wires were strung, and electricity was replacing candles and oil lamps as a light source as well as providing power for factory machinery. Still photography, invented before the Civil War, had evolved into moving pictures, which were eventually illuminated and projected by electricity.

The West had missed out on much of the huge surge of industrialization that had taken place to the east in the run-up to 1900. But by the turn of the twentieth century, it was as if the greater Los Angeles area was making up for lost time in its development. The region's speculators were on a mission, committed to growth and prosperity—specifically *their* prosperity—at an unprecedented pace. In 1880 the Los Angeles region's population was about 11,000; in 1890 it had grown to 50,000; by 1900 it had doubled again to just north of 100,000. Oil had been discovered in the region in 1892 and by the time of the vote in 1923 to determine if Beverly Hills would annex itself to Los Angeles, the region was providing a quarter of the world's oil output. Manufacturing had followed on the heels of the discovery of oil. By 1900, before water from the Owens Valley started to flow into the city through the Los Angeles Aqueduct in 1913, William Mulholland, as head of what would become the Los Angeles Department of Water and Power, was wresting enough water from the rivers and groundwater resources within the city limits for the municipal water supply to power this exponential growth.[7]

The land that had once been Maria Rita's Rancho de las Aguas and would become Beverly Hills was purchased from Hammel and Denker's heirs in 1900 by the Amalgamated Oil Company, a partnership that included some of the region's wealthiest citizens: oilmen and real estate developers Charles A. Canfield, Burton Green, and Max Whittier; railroad magnate Henry E. Huntington; and businessman William G. Kerckhoff. The idea was to drill for oil, in spite of the fact that owners during the previous fifty years, including Wilson and Hancock, who had bought the land from Maria Valdez, had searched for oil and failed to find it (or failed to find enough to make it economically feasible to start a full-scale drilling operation).

Amalgamated Oil dubbed its purchase Morocco Junction—no doubt a nod to Hammel and Denker's subdivision idea—and began drilling. They weren't any more successful than the previous owners in finding abundant deposits of oil, but they did find groundwater. With water seemingly plentiful (the partners realized that although there would not be enough water to sustain a new residential development far into the future, there was enough to get started), in 1906 Green and his partners reorganized into the Rodeo Land and Water Company and entered the world of land development. Beverly Hills was born.

The partners who made up the Rodeo Land and Water Company were businessmen who kept their eyes and ears open and were quick to seize opportunities. They were in it for the money, the more the better. If, along the way, enrichment brought a better social position and more influence, that was fine. They weren't averse to wielding the influence wealth brought, but their motivation wasn't to become famous, it was to get rich. They were certainly a mercenary lot, but not inherently bad, extraordinarily venal, or particularly nasty. If they suffered from any of the seven deadly sins, it was greed.

Burton Green, the principal in the Rodeo Land and Water Company who lived the longest, tends to get the lion's share of the credit for founding Beverly

Hills. But it was Charles Canfield, backed by fellow oil-man Max Whittier, and railroad magnate Henry E. Huntington, the company's largest stockholder, who were the initial driving forces behind the development. It was Henry Huntington who kick-started the idea of a residential development on the land that had been a bust as an oil field[8] by placing an ad in the October 21, 1906, edition of the *Los Angeles Times*. According to notes of a 1946 conversation on the history of Beverly Hills, the first city engineer, Arthur Pillsbury, stated it was Canfield who decreed that the new development would feature the best of everything.[9] That sentiment to strive for excellence and beauty on Canfield's part may have stemmed from his own personal tragedy: His wife had been murdered by a household employee at their Los Angeles home in 1902—in front of the couple's youngest daughter. Canfield was not at home at the time, he was in Mexico with Edward Doheny drilling for oil.[10] (Doheny's life would also be visited by murder in later years when, in the wake of the infamous Teapot Dome Scandal—when the administration of Warren G. Harding sold leased government petroleum reserves to private oil companies without competitive bidding in exchange for suitcases full of cash—his son, Ned, and an employee would both be shot through their heads in what was ruled a murder-suicide.) Regardless of whether Canfield's tragedy inspired his no-expense-spared approach to creating the new city, all the men of the Rodeo Land and Water Company were business success stories in the truest sense. They were canny, visionary, and had extraordinarily good timing. While they all certainly had outsized egos, they managed to stay focused on their shared goal. They knew the ropes of Southern California speculation and they knew each other—all of them had had business dealings with one or more of their fellow partners in the preceding years. Burton Green and Max Whittier had founded the Green & Whittier Oil Company, which had merged with other oil companies in which Charles Canfield and William G. Kerckhoff had stakes to become one of the largest petroleum concerns of the time, Associated Oil Company. Henry Huntington knew that to make his considerable investment in Rodeo Land and Water pay off, he would have to make sure people could get there on one of his rail lines. Easy to do when you are the titan of Southern California transportation: A light rail line to Beverly Hills was built.

Land speculation may have been familiar territory to Green and his partners, but as a residential community, Beverly Hills was a unique proposition from the get-go. In addition to a commitment to luxury, it was one of the first communities to be planned before ground had even been broken.[11] The company hired landscape architect Wilbur David Cook, who early in his career had worked with the famed Frederick Law Olmsted on many projects, including the White House grounds, to design a garden-inspired city. So instead of streets laid out in a grid, the roads of Beverly Hills were designed to be curvilinear, resembling, some said, early silent screen siren Theda Bara's torso. Each of the residential streets was lined with one variety of tree, reinforcing the park-like setting. In other, more regrettable ways, Beverly Hills followed the lead of other communities by including covenants, conditions, and restrictions (CC&R) in deeds for its lots that prevented non-Caucasians and Jews from owning, leasing, inheriting, or renting in the city.

The most frequently referenced urban legend as to where Beverly Hills got its name is that Green named it for his hometown of Beverly Farms, Massachusetts. A nice story, but it's not true. Green was from Wisconsin. Another version of the story is that Green got the idea for the city's name from reading a newspaper article about then-president William Howard Taft's summer White House in Beverly, Massachusetts, and thought "Beverly" was a pretty name. Except that Taft didn't take office until 1909, after the city had been named. Further urban legend has it that Green's wife, the former Lillian Wellburn, upon noting the topography, contributed "Hills." In fact, how Messrs. Green, Canfield, Whittier, and their fellow partners in the Rodeo Land and Water Company and their respective spouses—if they were involved at all—conjured up the city's name will probably remain a mystery.

2

The Beverly Hills Hotel and the Birth of Its Namesake City

⸻ ◇◇◇ ⸻

There must have been something about Beverly Hills in its earliest days that attracted strong women. Margaret Anderson was a force to be reckoned with almost a decade before Mary Pickford married Douglas Fairbanks and moved to Beverly Hills. There are those who say that Mrs. Anderson as much as anyone—and many who say *more* than anyone—was instrumental in making Beverly Hills a success.

Because in building the Beverly Hills Hotel, Mrs. Anderson gave the city a heart before it even had much of a body.

Although the city may have been imagined with

aspirations of luxury and high-minded intent, Beverly Hills was far from an overnight success. In fact, real estate sales were slow to the point of nonexistent. As of 1910—nine years before Doug Fairbanks bought the hunting lodge that would evolve into Pickfair—only six homes had been built north of Santa Monica Boulevard, the area of the city where the planners had created spacious lots. It was not a sustainable pace even for investors interested in the long game.

One of the challenges facing the young city was its remoteness. In an era when there were few cars in private hands and most people depended on horses and public transportation—trains, trolleys, and buses—Beverly Hills was difficult to get to. The only public transportation was provided by one of Henry Huntington's Los Angeles Pacific Railway "Dinky" lines—and Morocco Station, as the stop in Beverly Hills was initially called, was the end of the line. The Rodeo Land and Water Company needed something that would shift eyes westward to its new development. It knew that without something special, something showy, the market for lots in Beverly Hills would remain cool and sales would continue to move at a glacial pace. Burton Green and his fellow developers needed something that would make the world—especially potential buyers—take notice. They needed a showpiece that would wow prospective homeowners as well as be a comfortable place for people to spend time while they shopped for lots, and eventually, where they conferred with architects and builders. Taking a page from what the folks in the young city of Hollywood had done to entice potential residents, Burton Green and his Rodeo Land and Water Company partners decided to build a hotel that would be a regional attraction. In fact, they took more than a page from the Hollywood Hotel: To realize their vision they enticed Margaret Anderson, who had been in charge of building and outfitting the Hollywood Hotel and turning it into one of the city's most popular destinations during the previous decade, to be in charge of the project.

Born Margaret Boag in 1859 in Cedar Rapids, Iowa, Margaret Anderson came to California in 1874 as a teenager with her family. At twenty she married Lewis C. Anderson, a Danish immigrant. In the following years the couple had two children, Ruth and Stanley, and they moved to Alhambra, a community in the San Gabriel Valley, to grow navel oranges. (Navel oranges had become a very big deal for Southern California in the last quarter of the nineteenth century. Packed in their brightly decorated wooden crates with fanciful packing labels, the Southern Pacific Railway whisked these juicy and seedless golden globes across the country. The oranges became edible ambassadors for the Southern California good life.)

Margaret was married for eight years before her divorce from Lewis Anderson. She must have had a very good reason for taking such drastic action because divorce in the late nineteenth century was practically akin to social suicide. After she found herself an independent woman with two small children to provide for, Margaret considered her options. And the options were pretty limited: Just about the only respectable course for a divorced woman to make a living was as a teacher or running a boardinghouse. Margaret attended Hanna Los Angeles College, a women's college in downtown Los Angeles. After completing her studies, she and a friend, who was also a former student, ran a family boardinghouse south of downtown Los Angeles. Most women in Margaret's situation would have been content to stick with running a successful boardinghouse, but she took what she had learned to the next level: a hotel. Margaret applied for the position of managing a luxury hotel that the founders of the soon-to-be new city of Hollywood wanted to build to attract residents to the area. (Interestingly, and not without irony, Harvey and Daeida Wilcox, who had purchased the land that would become Hollywood, originally envisioned an enclave for Christian teetotalers.) Margaret helmed the project, working with the architects to realize a forty-room, mission-style building that would become the social center of the new city. The hotel opened on December 18, 1902. In 1903, Hollywood incorporated into an independent city. Not one to rest on her laurels, over the next eight years, Margaret saw to the purchase of land for expansion, hired architects to design the new space, and eventually grew the Hollywood Hotel to 114 bedrooms and the physical plant to include electricity, refrigeration, and a large boiler room.

In a time when many up-and-comers felt the need to cultivate pretensions, Margaret Anderson did not. She was not a snob. She had a keen eye that saw potential regardless of outward appearances. All were welcomed at the Hollywood Hotel and that included a young man who had taken a break from his architectural practice to work as a solo ranch hand on a spread in the young city of Hollywood. Instead of rattling around in the owner's empty ranch house in his off hours, Elmer Grey wanted to take his Sunday dinners at Margaret's establishment. The hotel's convivial atmosphere and Margaret's cordial mien prompted Grey to ask her if he could spend his evenings sitting in the lobby. According to Margaret, it most certainly was all right and Grey most certainly did spend a great deal of time at the hotel. He went on to make a circle of friends. When he became a subject of gossip because he was "a hired hand by day and assumed equal at night,"[1] a young woman with secure social status who was one of his friends gave a formal ball, invited Grey, and gave him the first two dances on her card.[2]

It would turn out to be an advantageous association for both Grey and Anderson. Learning that Grey was an architect, Margaret Anderson would go on to hire him to design the expansion of the Hollywood Hotel and draw up the plans for the Beverly Hills Hotel. Margaret's methodology of building a network of interesting, talented people based on her instincts instead of their outward appearances might not have worked in many places with aspirations of high society, but it would be just the ticket for running the most important establishment in the early days of the new city of Beverly Hills.

The Rodeo Land and Water Company knew what it was doing when it directed its agents to approach Mrs. Anderson to see to the creation of a luxury hotel for its new city, and it had the good sense not to stint on the enticements. The deal included prime land atop a hillside in the new development—which provided the needed drainage, a problem that had plagued the Hollywood Hotel—that was located near a steady source of water, a generous budget to build and outfit the new hotel, as well as the guarantee that no other hotel would open in Beverly Hills for the following thirteen years. And the principals of the Rodeo Land and Water Company weren't disappointed. Margaret, along with her son Stanley Anderson, who had learned the ropes of running a hotel through on-the-job training from his mother, delivered and then some. Once Margaret came on board with the project, it was full steam ahead. Under her direction the region's best architects, including her old friend Elmer Grey, and builders were hired and set on a pace that saw the hotel completed in just over a year. Upon completion, the new hotel could not have opened in a more dramatic fashion. Before breakfast on the morning of April 30, 1912, guests staying at the Hollywood Hotel, of which Mrs. Anderson had remained manager while the new hotel was being built, were informed the building was closing. The entire staff then decamped for the new Beverly Hills Hotel with many of the guests following, finding on arrival that the new facility was ready for them. It was the sort of grand stunt that would set the promotional tone for the city for decades to come.

Newspapers across the country picked up the story. Practically before a single guest had spent the night at the new hotel, it was famous. This was no small accomplishment. In spite of its distance from the East

Coast's population centers, the Los Angeles region wasn't lacking in luxury hotels. Several establishments had opened in the last three decades of the nineteenth century, including the Pico House in downtown Los Angeles and Pasadena's Hotel Raymond and Hotel Green, as well as the aforementioned Hollywood Hotel, which opened just after the turn of the twentieth century.

It's almost impossible to underestimate the significance of the Beverly Hills Hotel in the success of Beverly Hills the city. Under Margaret Anderson's watch, the hotel would become much more than a respite for prospective residents, some of whom stayed for extended periods of time. It would become the heart and soul of the new city. In its early days, the hotel was the center for both indoor entertainment, like movies and concerts, and outdoor pursuits, including riding and golf at the neighboring Los Angeles Country Club, as well as a school and place of worship, not to mention restaurants that served meals on a daily basis and sumptuous feasts at holidays.

And the hotel did its job. Sales for property in Beverly Hills picked up. Construction on homes commenced. The population, while not exploding, increased. Families moved in, and in addition to attending classes held at the Beverly Hills Hotel, students began to show up at the area's one existing school, the old Canyon School, a one-room school-house built in 1887, located at the bottom of Coldwater Canyon.

It was over what the residents considered needed improvements of the Canyon School that one of the first tensions between the community of Beverly Hills and the City and County of Los Angeles began to brew, becoming the first step toward Beverly Hills' incorporation as a separate city. In 1913, Beverly Hills requested that the Los Angeles City Council expand the school. Los Angeles turned them down. Beverly Hills' residents decided to hold an election to vote on a resolution to create a separate school district. After being passed, a board of trustees was formed. Until the city was incorporated the following year, the Rodeo Land and Water Company picked up the tab for the new school, which had been relocated to what is now the corner of Coldwater Canyon and Sunset Boulevard.[3]

In early 1914, two years after the Beverly Hills Hotel opened its doors and a year after the community's first skirmish with the City of Los Angeles over the needed improvements at Canyon School, Beverly Hills incorporated as a general law city of the sixth class[4] under California law, giving it the power to levy taxes as well as the responsibility to provide services such as police, fire, schools, and zoning, and enabling it to issue building permits—for which it could collect fees. At the time of incorporation, the city didn't have quite enough residents within its borders to technically qualify as a general law city of the sixth class, so Rodeo Land and Water Company principal Henry Huntington, who had men to spare on his payroll, sent in ringers by rail to make up the needed numbers. Considering how fast and loose politicians of the era played with what laws there were, it was a mild chicanery.

From almost the beginning, the relationship between the City of Beverly Hills and the Rodeo Land and Water Company was an uncomfortable fit. The newborn city was well aware that the Rodeo Land and Water Company paid 70 percent of the taxes it levied and knew that what was in the best interest of the company wasn't necessarily in the best interest of the city.[5] Contractually obligated to provide municipal services, Rodeo separated its real estate and water businesses the year the city incorporated, founding the Beverly Hills Utility Company. Water, sewers, and trash collection would become the responsibility of the new Utility Company; Rodeo Land and Water would continue to sell land.

The men who created Beverly Hills didn't set out to build a residential haven for the stars of the silver screen who were beginning to call the region home.

In fact, if the recollections of the Beverly Hills first city engineer, Arthur Pillsbury, are correct, it was the opposite: So pervasive were the negative feeling toward "picture folk" throughout the region, that originally, agents were *not* supposed to sell to anyone in the movie business.[6] But if the likes of Mary Pickford, Douglas Fairbanks, and Charlie Chaplin wanted to buy some of the city's most expensive lots and build on them, and the city reaped the considerable publicity of the stars residing within its borders, it turned out to be perfectly all right with Beverly Hills' creators. (It is said at least one of the original residents of the area, who predated cityhood, complained about "picture folk" moving in. According to local legend, it was hotelier Stanley Anderson who talked this nervous Nellie down off the ledge.)[7] "Picture folk" were part of the future for the young, affluent city. Call it providential timing or just coincidence, but at the same time real estate development in Beverly Hills was gaining traction, the film industry was becoming solidly entrenched in and around Hollywood. And this parallel growth should not have been a surprise to the principals in the Rodeo Land and Water Company. Green especially was more than aware that moviemaking was on track to become a permanent fixture in the region; he had been involved in the sale of a vast tract of land in the San Fernando Valley to

Carl Laemmle that would become Universal Studios. Ditto a similar sentiment on the parts of Margaret and Stanley Anderson. The Hollywood Hotel had become a popular way station and watering hole for the vanguard members of the motion picture industry, newly transplanted from New York. It might be farther afield than other Los Angeles–area neighborhoods, but Beverly Hills had the potential to be the perfect place for the newly minted stars of the silver screen to settle down. It wouldn't be long before that came to pass.

3

Setting the Stage

———◇◇———

In the first decade and a half of the twentieth century, as the Rodeo Land and Water Company was busy speculating in land and seeking to extract natural resources from under the ground, the movie stars who would one day live in the brand spanking new development were just getting their start in an industry that was fresh off its Big Bang in New York City.

The business of moving pictures was an open playing field for whomever had the moxie to take a chance. And the men who initially took those chances—the men who would eventually be the founders of the Hollywood "industry"—were Eastern European Jewish immigrants. At the end of the nineteenth century, it wasn't such a difficult business to get into. The stakes weren't very high at the beginning, when moving pictures were a cheap leisure-time activity for immigrants and the working class. It was an accessible business opportunity for the Jewish immigrants because the white Anglo-Saxon Protestant business establishment had scant interest in a diversion associated with what was perceived as the lower orders of society. The Jews who did go into the moving picture business and went on to become the founding fathers of Hollywood's movie industry, such as Adolph Zukor, had other advantages over WASP businessmen: Working in retail and fashion, as Zukor had done earlier in his career, had given them experience in recognizing trends and identifying what would become popular. And, finally, since the WASPs weren't interested in the nascent business of moving pictures, there were no social barriers preventing Jews from entering the field. It's not without reason that when Adolph Zukor visited a penny arcade in 1903, as he told Michael Korda when reminiscing about how he got started, "I looked around and said, 'A Jew could make a lot of money at this.'"[1]

What Zukor saw in the arcade were peep shows—not peep shows in the prurient sense, but machines where an individual could look through a viewfinder while turning a hand crank to flip through a series of photos that constituted a moving picture scene. The medium was still a ways off from audiences seated in auditoriums viewing projected ten-minute single and double reelers, let alone multi-reel features. New York was the center for these arcades, many of which were started by men like Adolph Zukor. Zukor would eventually start Famous Players, the company for which Mary Pickford would work for many years. Famous Players later merged with Jesse Lasky's company in 1916, becoming the architects of what we know today collectively as Hollywood.

It took a few years to transition from arcades with individual peep show machines to the concept of a "movie" as something audiences sat down and engaged with like a play. But the men who had invested in the arcades were in an advantageous position to transition to exhibiting films when the time came. They already had the locations; transforming a penny arcade to a movie theater required a minimal renovation that involved removing the peep show machines, installing seats, and obtaining a projector. The added bonus: They could charge a nickel per showing, hence the moniker "nickelodeon" for the early movie theaters. Some of the Eastern European Jews who began in the moving picture business in New York at the turn of the twentieth century would go on to establish empires that revolved around exhibiting films in grander and grander movie palaces, others would shift into creating the films that were shown, and a few would do it all.

It isn't surprising that the developing moving picture industry, and the technology that supported it, got its start in New York City. It was, after all, the most populous city in the United States with the largest potential audiences that included seemingly endless fresh waves of immigrants, the country's financial center, and, maybe most importantly, the center of theater, which provided some of the raw material for moving pictures—such as actors, directors, set directors, and lighting experts. Not that those early moving pictures *were* theater, which had taken on an elevated status of Culture with a capital "C," but rather an entertaining diversion for immigrants and the lower classes. Those early flickers were immensely popular, though. Within ten years of the turn of the century there were studios churning out moving pictures in every borough of New York and across the Hudson River in New Jersey (Fort Lee, New Jersey, was the moving picture capital of the United States at this time).

History is full of "what ifs." A case could be made that if Thomas Edison had not been so zealous about enforcing his patents for the technology that enabled the filming and subsequent exhibiting of moving pictures, if he hadn't been so committed to building and sustaining the vertical monopoly he cultivated first as an individual, then as The Edison Trust, and finally as the force behind the Motion Picture Patents Company (MPPC), if he had been less rigid about licensing his inventions and open to the creative ideas of others, the motion picture industry might have stayed in and around New York City and not have made the wholesale move to Southern California.

But Edison, the man and then the eponymous trust followed by the grandiose-sounding MPPC, spent considerable time, energy, and money sending agents out to patrol the New York City environs, seeking out the scofflaws who were using his equipment and not paying him for the privilege to do so.

By its second decade of existence, invention, reinvention, and innovation was already sweeping through the movie business. While the producers and Edison's MPPC were doing battle, another revolution was taking place in the world of filmmaking: Stars were being born. Unlike legitimate theater, which featured cast members on the marquee, for the most part actors and actresses in the early days of moving pictures went unbilled. Chief among these new stars/celebrities was Mary Pickford, who had created a demand for herself starting in 1909 by making fifty-one films for the Biograph Company in the course of a year.

Pickford would evolve from "The Biograph Girl" and "The Girl with the Golden Curls" to Mary Pickford, "America's Sweetheart" and, not incidentally, the highest-paid film actor of her time. She would eventually move from Biograph to Zukor and Lasky's Famous Players-Lasky Corporation.

And then Southern California beckoned.

The conventional wisdom is that the industry picked up stakes and moved across the continent for the light and the weather. That is far from the whole story. While the more clement weather was an attractive benefit, the move west was also a financial and creative reaction to Thomas Edison's heavy-handed enforcement of the patents he controlled, including those for almost all of the early cameras and projectors. The West Coast was a five-day train ride away from Edison's purview, and although he periodically sent representatives on cross-country train rides to investigate patent infringements, by the time these men arrived at the Los Angeles train station, the filmmakers, having received advance warning, would have packed up their cameras and headed the 120 miles to Mexico, where Edison's patents couldn't be enforced.

It was to Hollywood in early 1910—on the cusp of becoming part of the larger city of Los Angeles after being an independent city for seven years—that D. W. Griffith brought moviemaking technicians and many of his regular retinue of actors, which included Lillian Gish, Lionel Barrymore, and Mary Pickford. He shot a number of films all over the Los Angeles area for Biograph, including the first moving picture shot in Hollywood, *In Old California*, a melodrama about the Rancho era when Alta California was part of Mexico, and *Love Among the Roses*, starring Mary Pickford, on the grounds of painter Paul de Longpré's then world-famous garden.

Although the Los Angeles area offered great weather—not only was there no snow, but the weather was warm enough to shoot out of doors even in February and March, something that was impossible in and around New York—and a wide variety of outdoor locations, including beaches, mountains, woods, and deserts, it didn't offer much in the way of man-made diversions. Something the troupe of young actors and moviemaking craftsmen must have noticed. Compared with New York, where Biograph shot its movies in a brownstone on East 14th Street, Los Angeles and Hollywood must have been a shock to their system. Even forays outside of New York City for exterior shots must have held more allure than Hollywood in the early days. There were day trips across the Hudson to the New Jersey countryside and longer shoots that involved train travel farther north into upstate New York. On those trips, the Biograph company would work all day in heavy costumes and party into the night with everything from cards and dice games to singing and reciting Shakespeare. That wouldn't be the case in Hollywood, which in 1910 was still a quiet village. After working all day the cast and crew would repair to Los Angeles, which was, in just about everyone's opinion, a dump. D. W. Griffith stayed at the Alexandria Hotel; Mary, always frugal to a fault, stayed in far less luxurious lodgings with her younger brother Jack, who was fifteen at the time, and a few other girls in the company.

Breaking free from the constraints of the East Coast, both legal and creative, and heading to Southern California brought its own set of challenges. What the motion picture workforce found when they arrived in the dry and dusty environs of Los Angeles was both a blessing and a curse for the new industry. Everyone from the nascent studio heads like Zukor, Lasky, Laemmle, and William Selig to the young actors, actresses, scene painters, camera operators, lighting technicians, and screenwriters (called scenarists at the time) found a young city with little of the urban infrastructure—such as paved streets, readily available public transportation, universal electrification, and easily accessible telegraphy facilities—they had taken for granted in New York.

Mary Pickford described that first trip to Hollywood in both her 1954 series of articles for *McCall's* and her subsequent 1955 autobiography, *Sunshine and Shadow*, this way:

"Our studio consisted of an acre of ground, fenced in, and a large wooden platform hung with cotton shades that were pulled on wires overhead. On a windy day our clothes and the curtains on the set would flap loudly in the breeze. Studios were all on open lots, roofless and without walls, which explains the origin of the term 'on the lot.' Dressing rooms being a non-existent luxury, we donned our costumes every morning at the hotel. Our rehearsal room was improvised from an office which Griffith rented in a decrepit old building on Main Street. A kitchen table and three chairs were all there was of furniture. Mr. Griffith occupied one of the chairs, the other being reserved for the elderly members of the cast. The rest of us sat on the floor."[2]

Mary left out the less salubrious bits from her recollections of her first trip to Southern California. Hollywood didn't exactly embrace the motion picture pioneers who had come west. In fact, the movie people received a pretty frigid reception from the city that would soon become the capital of American filmmaking. The city's citizens complained long and loud about the first filmmakers. In addition to the people, who Hollywood residents had determined were a totally disreputable crowd, the film itself stank up the place. Silver nitrate film smelled bad, especially when the exposed footage of cut scenes and rejected takes was burned to reclaim the silver. Film stock presented a danger as well—it was notoriously flammable and buildings that housed it were always in danger of burning to a crisp. The landlords of Hollywood did their best to discourage what they perceived as a crowd of ne'er-do-wells with pyromaniac tendencies who made up the filmmaking community from renting in the city. "No Movies" accompanied "No Dogs" as prohibitions on "For Rent" signs and in newspaper advertisements.[3] And it wasn't just the making of movies to which Hollywood's citizens objected; going to the moving pictures was just as unpopular. Most of Hollywood's residents avoided The Idle Hour, the city's one movie theater, which opened in 1910. In a God-fearing, teetotaling community like Hollywood, idleness was not something to be encouraged.

To those who had lived in more established cities, the backwardness of the urban amenities of Los Angeles, Hollywood, Long Beach, and Santa Monica came as a shock. What was also a surprise to the moviemakers was the small-minded smugness of the residents, the vast majority of whom had arrived within the previous ten years. The Anglo population that moved into the region had dragged along the same prejudices about religion, class, and ethnic background that were a fact of life on the East Coast. Even though the region had only been part of the United States since 1850, after being part of Spain and then Mexico for more than three centuries, it was as if the Americans who moved in wanted to purge the region of any influence of its former Mexican identity. The new power structure, which included transportation barons and land and oil speculators, wanted to re-create the white, Christian environments they had left behind in the East and the Midwest, even if those places existed only in their imaginations. The only saving grace for the newcomers who worked in the moving picture business was that in the second decade of the twentieth century there just wasn't a large enough population of citizens who fancied themselves of such high moral standard that they were in a position to judge "picture folk" and to carry through wholesale discrimination on a consistent basis, which isn't to say they didn't try. That, and land speculators would sell to almost anyone if it meant turning a buck. Well, anyone who was white.

The Hollywood of the early twentieth century was a far cry from what it ultimately became just a few decades later. It was founded as a God-fearing community by devout Christians and teetotalers Harvey and Daeida Wilcox. Harvey, originally a cobbler, had made a fortune in real estate in Topeka, Kansas, where he met Daeida. After the couple married around 1883, they headed west on the recently completed rail line that ran directly to Los Angeles. Before long Harvey Wilcox had set up a real estate office and entered the growing field of land speculation just in time for one of the region's many real estate booms between 1886 and 1889. The couple began buying parcels of land in what was known as the Cahuenga Valley. Harvey made a map of his new subdivision, naming the ruler-straight streets he had drawn that crossed each other in a neat perpendicular grid. Daeida supplied the name Hollywood after a visit to her native Ohio. A woman she fell into conversation with on her trip told Daeida that her estate in Illinois was named "Hollywood." Daeida liked the name and so did Harvey: Hollywood it was.[4]

Although the couple made frequent trips to the property they had purchased, much of which had been planted with citrus orchards, they didn't live there at first. Then, when the region's boom transformed into one of its frequent busts, the couple was forced to sell their fancy house in Los Angeles and move to more modest accommodations in their subdivision. It might have been the best thing that happened to the development on its way to cityhood. Before he lived on his property Harvey Wilcox was prevented by law from grading roads. Once he actually lived on his land, road building could commence. Wells were dug and windmills were built. Larger landowners dug deeper wells equipped with gasoline-powered pumps. Groves of orange, lemon, olive, and fig trees grew.

In 1891 Harvey died, but his widow persevered in the development she had named. Eventually land values began to rise again and lots began to sell. In 1903, Hollywood, with a population of seven hundred, became an independent city (only men voted). The very first law that was passed banned the sale of alcohol—no surprise considering the teetotaling founders. More laws quickly followed, including some that banned the transport of alcohol through the city, concealed firearms, bicycles on the sidewalks (interesting, since sidewalks in the young city were few and far between), pool halls, bowling alleys, slot machines, and gambling of any sort. Hollywood was a serious, sober, God-fearing city with no bars, hotels forbidden to serve alcohol, and little in the way of entertainment.[5] What few businesses existed were closed by 10:30 p.m. every night and all day Sunday.

It may have been dull, but it was pleasant. For the seven years Hollywood was an independent city it was a bit of a rural wonderland for its residents. Wealthy Midwesterners built winter homes on large lots. Even John Toberman, who spent six years as the mayor of Los Angeles, built a home there. (The mayor's nephew, C. E. Toberman, saw the potential of selling land to the moving picture industry earlier than most. He marketed the vacant land he owned to the nascent studios by advertising "Hollywood is at the threshold of a new era of development.")[6] Surrounding the homes were orchards. It was a city of "rural refinement," according to Gregory Paul Williams' *The Story of Hollywood: An Illustrated History.* Until, that is, it wasn't anymore.

By 1910 it was clear to Hollywood's municipal officials that the city could not sustain itself. Hollywood had a problem with drainage and, eventually, sewage disposal. Mud and debris would pour down from the hillsides into Hollywood during the rainy season, flooding streets and disrupting public transportation by burying the rail lines. Property owners who wanted to subdivide didn't want to accommodate the need for septic tanks. And, of course, the more people who moved into Hollywood, coupled with the number of orchards, the greater the strain on the already limited amount of available groundwater. The idea of joining the city of Los Angeles, which had been anathema to the early denizens of Hollywood, began to seem more appealing. Encouraged by land speculators, including General Harrison Gray Otis and Harry Chandler of the *Los Angeles Times*, both of whom had skin in the game in William Mulholland's endeavor to bring water from the Owens Valley to Los Angeles—water which, it had been made clear, would not be shared with other cities—Hollywood succumbed to what seemed like its inevitable fate and voted itself out of existence. Flush with the anticipation of all that free-flowing water, Los Angeles was like the kid who owned the ball: The game would be played by their rules. The sole concession to Hollywood's teetotalers was a continued ban on the sale of alcohol, a concession that would not last long. Like most of the coastal basin, Hollywood and its neighboring city of Colegrove were absorbed into the evolving megacity of Los Angeles. It may have seemed like a good idea at the time, especially considering the anticipation of water that would be available when Mulholland's Owens Valley project was completed in three years' time. But in short order taxes and assessments levied on property by Los Angeles made continuing to maintain citrus orchards impractical. Agriculture and "rural refinement" as a way of life segued into residential subdivisions and movie studios. As part of Los Angeles, in the coming decades Hollywood would be unable to protect itself from the larger city's urban blight.

In her recollections of the time, Mary Pickford makes no mention of any negative reception she and her fellow Biograph coworkers encountered in that first foray to "The Coast." While D. W. Griffith and his troupe of actors went about their business, making a number of films throughout the region during the four months they were in the Los Angeles area, the preternaturally observant young Mary Pickford cannot have helped but notice the contempt in which movie folk were held by the locals even though the Biograph team kept to themselves. For example, to pass the time when the Biograph players weren't actually filming, Griffith would encourage them to come up with stories. Mary came up with two right away and Biograph paid for both: For the first one, which she recalls was the outline of Jules Massenet's opera *Thaïs*, she received $10; for the second, *May and December*, she received $15.[7]

While the reception from the residents of Hollywood might have been less than welcoming, on the other side of the coin, when Mary Pickford returned to New York, she and her brother Jack presented their mother with a black leather handbag. Inside were twenty-four crisp, new $50 bills. Charlotte Pickford had never seen a $50 bill; she thought at first it was stage money. In 2016 dollars, that $1,200 was the equivalent of more than $30,000. It was these earnings from her first working trip to Hollywood that Mary felt were the beginnings of affluence for the Pickford family. Mary always watched the bottom line. When she added it all up, Hollywood equaled financial security.

If Mary Pickford had somehow missed the cool-to-hostile reception she and her Biograph cohorts encountered in 1910, when she returned to Los Angeles in 1913 with her mother, the treatment her fellow moving picture folk received cannot have escaped her notice. (Mary had married fellow Biograph actor Owen Moore in 1911 in New York, but by the time of her return to Southern California, she was already living apart from him.) Mary Pickford was already a movie star, though the term hadn't yet been coined, so she and Charlotte Pickford moved into comfortable digs, a Craftsman-style bungalow on Western Avenue. For others who lacked fame and its companion, fortune, landlords were less generous. Prospective tenants were greeted with signs informing them: No Jews. No Dogs. No "Movie."[8]

The love-hate relationship Hollywood—and Los

Angeles, of which the former city was now a part—developed with the industry that would go on to define the region to the world was beginning to solidify when Douglas Fairbanks hit town in July 1915 to film Griffith's *The Lamb*. Fresh from Broadway, he had his first wife, son, and entourage in tow. (Fairbanks did not travel light; his excess baggage fees totaled $52.44, about $1,250 in 2016 dollars.) Fairbanks, who had made a point of emphasizing in the press that he was a man of the "legitimate" theater, meaning Broadway, had danced around the emerging world of the flickers for a number of years, talking to producers, having screen tests, and waiting for the right (read: most lucrative) moment. When they arrived, the Fairbanks family stayed at one of Los Angeles' finest hotels, The Alexandria (where D. W. Griffith had stayed in 1910 on his first foray to film in Hollywood), before leasing a two-story home on North Highland Avenue in Hollywood.[9] Although renowned as being insouciant and high-spirited, Fairbanks was acutely sensitive to being half-Jewish. Overt anti-Semitism was the order of the day. The "No Dogs. No Movie" signs placed by landlords on buildings and in newspaper advertisements may have escaped Fairbanks' notice, but it's more than reasonable to expect he saw the words "No Jews."

The antipathy exhibited by the neighborhood is

especially curious considering Hollywood did not have much else in the pipeline to generate business at the time moviemaking started to grow. For the first decade of the twentieth century, the home and gardens of French painter Paul de Longpré had been enough of a tourist draw to boost occupancy at the city's few hotels. With de Longpré's death in 1911, that more genteel attraction to outsiders ended and nearby hotels faced ruin. While land speculator C. E. Toberman welcomed the new industry—and its pocketbook—with open arms, his more fastidious neighbors held their collective noses.

In 1911, not long after Griffith wound up his months-long stay in the area, David and William Horsley moved their Nestor Studios from Bayonne, New Jersey, to the Los Angeles area. Hollywood was in business and an industry was born. And what a business it was. The way studios were springing up all over the region was dizzying. Within three months of Nestor Studios opening, there were fifteen or so more studios in Hollywood. "Studio" being a relative term, since many of the companies shooting Westerns, comedies, and melodramas were as Mary Pickford described: open lots with an elevated platform shielded by large white curtains hung on wires so they could be adjusted to filter the sun. Even studios that had come west to the region before Nestor set up shop, like Brooklyn-based Vitagraph, shuttered their studio in Santa Monica and moved to Hollywood. It was during this period that some of the actors who would join Mary Pickford in her battle against Beverly Hills' annexation to Los Angeles came to Hollywood, including Harold Lloyd and Tom Mix.

4

A Crash Course in Influence

———◇◈◇———

I t could be argued that nothing less cataclysmic than America's entry into World War One was the first step toward the eventual relocation of Douglas Fairbanks and, after their marriage, Mary Pickford to Beverly Hills. Even though Mary and Doug's affair had started in 1916 while the pair were working in New York City, when the United States entered the war in 1917 both were living in homes on either end of Hollywood, married to other people. There is absolutely no doubt that their support of the war effort on behalf of the U.S. government was sincere, but the silver lining was that their patriotic cheerleading enabled them to appear together in public cloaked in the innocence of their good intentions. The subterfuge worked, but only for a while.

If their popularity with audiences helped Mary Pickford and Douglas Fairbanks learn how to negotiate higher and higher salaries with the studio chiefs, it was the Orwellian-sounding Committee for Public Information (CPI), established in 1917 as the government's department of propaganda to sell World War One to the public, as well as the Department of the Treasury under Secretary William McAdoo, that showed them just how influential they could be in the world at large. In fact, for Pickford, Fairbanks, Charlie Chaplin, and others, working with the CPI to make movies and with the U.S. Department of the Treasury to sell Liberty Bonds during World War One was their on-the-job training for how to influence crowds of people into doing something that, left to their own devices, they probably wouldn't.

President Woodrow Wilson had a problem that extended beyond the drumbeats of war coming from Europe. Through the early days of World War One, his primary foreign policy goal had been to keep the United States out of the hostilities. When Wilson ran for his second term in 1916, it was on a platform of U.S. neutrality. Even at the time, though, Wilson must have known that staying out of the war was like whistling by the graveyard. By 1915 it had become clear that it was going to prove difficult if not impossible for the United States to avoid entering the fray. Great

Britain declared a naval blockade of ships from neutral countries going to Germany; Germany declared the waters around Great Britain a war zone with no guarantees of safety for ships flying the flags of neutral countries. By 1915 Germany was sinking ships flying under American flags, including passenger ships. In May 1915, the British liner RMS *Lusitania* was torpedoed, sinking off the coast of Ireland. Many of the more than one thousand victims who lost their lives were Americans. Three strongly worded diplomatic protests to the Germans were rebuffed. It was becoming clear to Wilson and other members of the government that the United States was going to have to come to the aid of its European allies England and France. Wilson's secretary of state, William Jennings Bryan, a pacifist, resigned and was replaced by Robert Lansing, an authority on international law who had been a special counsel to the State Department. In 1916, Wilson requested appropriations for 500,000 troops and a buildup of naval vessels that included battleships, cruisers, destroyers, and submarines.

President Wilson's primary domestic challenge in the months before he was certain that the United States would have to go to war was to inform the country's citizens and get them on board. Every student in U.S. schools learns about the great American melting pot. But in the second decade of the twentieth century, the "pot" was more along the lines of swirling ingredients that hadn't yet mixed let alone "melted" together. And one of those components was a large population of German descent, many of whom had been born in Germany or were first-generation Americans. The government had to calibrate a consistent and uniform message to encourage patriotism while at the same time discouraging allegiances to the old country; they had to provide a message that addressed the government's seeming contradiction of turning from neutrality to taking up arms. And the government had to navigate the potential land mines of freedom of the press while quashing dissent.

Enter George Creel. On April 13, 1917, a week after the United States formally entered the war, President Wilson created the Committee on Public Information. He asked Denver newsman George Creel to head the new civilian agency based on a memo Creel had sent the president about "expression, not suppression" of the press. Rather than put the screws on freedom of the press, not unexpected during times of war, Creel was proposing to spin the press; he suggested using the "carrot" approach of providing packaged news reports to newspapers around the country with the understanding that if these reports weren't accepted, the "stick" of censorship would be sure to follow. According to *Words That Won the War: The Story of the Committee on Public Information, 1917–1919*, by James R. Mock and Cedric Larson:

"The Committee on Public Information was assigned the staggering task of 'holding fast the inner lines.' The story of how it fulfilled that mission is a dramatic record of vigor, effectiveness, and creative imagination. The Committee was America's 'propaganda ministry' during the World War, charged with encouraging and then consolidating the revolution of opinion, which changed the United States from antimilitaristic democracy to an organized war machine. This work touched the private life of virtually every man, woman, and child; it reflected the thoughts of the American people under the leadership of Woodrow Wilson; and it popularized what was for us a new idea of the individual's relation to the state."[1]

Consider the challenge: Reaching out to the country's widespread population with a consistent message was a tall order; even radio, which seems like ancient technology today, didn't begin until 1920 when KDKA sent out its first broadcast. Radio networks wouldn't exist for another six years after that. And even though there was an ongoing shift in population from rural to urban at the time, large numbers of people still lived on farms miles from the closest village or town. Daily papers weren't delivered to remote farms, and the local weekly papers that were common in rural areas weren't timely enough, plus there was no guarantee that they would be read, or that they *could* be read. In 1917 there was still a surprising number of people who were illiterate. A large number of these citizens lived too far afield to attend patriotic rallies put on by local organizations. But by 1917, millions of Americans were going to the picture shows, many on a weekly basis. They frequented movie theaters religiously and watched Mary Pickford, Douglas Fairbanks, Charlie Chaplin, Roscoe "Fatty" Arbuckle, Tom Mix, Lillian and Dorothy Gish, and Mabel Normand week after week after week. It was, in every respect, a captive audience and a perfect opportunity for the government to deliver its wartime messages. George Creel's committee had an incredibly effective delivery vehicle designed to fill in the approximately four minutes it took to change the film reels on the projector: For each venue, the committee would tap a community leader, known as a Four Minute Man, to stand before the audience and deliver the weekly message on the war. The Four Minute Men, drawn mostly from local lawyers and bankers, men comfortable with delivering messages in a succinct way—as opposed to orators such as clergymen who loved the sound of their own voices and rarely adhered to admonitions of brevity—would prepare weekly addresses relating to the war based on topics provided by Creel's committee. Admonished to hold the audiences' attention, keep overt partisanship at bay, maintain restraint, and exhibit good manners, the men conveyed news on such topics as the Liberty Loan program, the national Red Cross Drive, conservation of food and fuel, and donations of binoculars to the navy. The CPI's central office issued bulletins suggesting topics and guidelines on how best to deliver the points. Creel's CPI went one step further: It sought and received the support of the National Association of the Motion Picture Industry, which named the Four Minute Men as the "official and authorized representatives of the United States Government in the movie theaters of America."[2] The program reached millions of people a week in a way that no other method could and the idea's effectiveness extended from remote rural areas into the cities. Each week in New York City alone, sixteen hundred Four Minute Men speaking in English, Yiddish, or Italian addressed more than half a million people. It was the first step in the relationship between the motion picture community and the war effort. There would be more.

In fact, no city was more patriotic and gung-ho than Hollywood. Mary Pickford, Douglas Fairbanks, and director D. W. Griffith led a Liberty parade on Hollywood Boulevard. Hollywood was the first community to oversubscribe its allotment of war bonds; Fairbanks alone spent $100,000.[3] The names of well-known actors may not have been on the lists of men being inducted into the armed services, but that didn't mean Hollywood wasn't throwing itself into the war effort. When the CPI came calling, asking for films with sympathetic story lines that reinforced the government's message that the war was worth the cost, Hollywood threw itself into the task. As Words That Won the War summarized:

"No field of entertainment felt the effect of war more strongly than the movies, and none was of greater interest to the CPI. . . . [The] movie film was both the easiest way of presenting propaganda in the form of entertainment and one of the important items in a broad program of civilian morale."[4]

It was a mutually beneficial partnership: Hollywood would make movies that the CPI would actively promote. The men at the helm of the movie companies relished their roles. In fact, the movie industry's War Cooperating Committee, which included William Fox, D. W. Griffith, Thomas H. Ince, Jesse L. Lasky, Carl Laemmle, Marcus Loew, Joseph M. Schenck, Lewis J. Selznick, and Adolph Zukor, traveled to Washington, D.C., in July 1917, to confer with each government department to learn how their industry could help. And it was the smart move as there was little doubt that lack of support and cooperation on the part of Hollywood could quickly translate to censorship—or worse. Films deemed as appealing to Anglophobes or pro-German, in other words "pro-peace," could be seized under Title XI of the recently enacted Espionage Act and producers could be tried and imprisoned. Making war movies wasn't going to make the studios rich—profits from the films were shared with the CPI—but Hollywood's enthusiastic participation would not only secure priceless government goodwill, but also make sure moving pictures had a positive place in the American psyche.

No one threw themselves into supporting the war effort through their work more than Mary Pickford. She starred in *The Little American,* proclaiming, "I used to be neutral till I saw your soldiers destroying women and shooting old men. Then I stopped being 'neutral' and became a human being!"[5] She was everywhere: In addition to leading the march through Hollywood, she appeared in the propaganda short *War Relief,* posed for posters, had photographs taken of her collecting cigarettes to send to the troops overseas, had others taken of her kissing the American flag, and led a Marine band through San Francisco. As the patron of a Red Cross unit, Mary Pickford signed the receipts that were sent back to donors. She was made an honorary colonel of the 143rd California

Field Artillery, who all wore her photo in a locket.[6] Mary Pickford was a one-woman war-support machine.

The jingoistic movies starring the world's most famous actors and actresses were serving their purpose. Creel and his fellow committee members were doing a superb job uniting the American population in support of the war thanks in large part to the movies they were seeing in theaters and the words of the Four Minute Men. But in spite of the slides being projected before and after each film exhorting Americans to buy Liberty Bonds, that program was lagging behind. Something more had to be done and Hollywood—specifically its biggest stars—would be the source of that "something."

William Gibbs McAdoo, as Woodrow Wilson's secretary of the Treasury (and son-in-law), was responsible for financing World War One, both stateside and through loans to America's allies. It certainly helped that the citizenry had been brought around and was in favor of American involvement in the European war, but that enthusiasm wasn't translating into robust sales of Liberty Bonds, which the government needed to finance the soldiers it was conscripting and all the munitions it was manufacturing. To proselytize the sale of bonds Secretary McAdoo would need a bold stroke, something more than including slides before feature presentations at movie theaters and asking community leaders and Four Minute Men to do their best to encourage their fellow citizens to buy bonds. So McAdoo did something that had never been done before: He called on stars of the moving pictures, people who, quite simply, were immensely popular and whose recognition transcended community, state, and even national borders, to spread the word. In retrospect, it was a genius move and must have seemed nothing short of revolutionary at the time. Movie stars had barely been invented, they certainly had never been called on by their government to lend their celebrity to a cause. In fairness to Secretary McAdoo, asking movie stars to lend a hand wasn't the only bold step he took while helming the Treasury Department. He also closed the New York Stock Market for four months to prevent Europeans from selling their stocks and bonds, converting the dollars they received from the sales to gold and destabilizing the American economy. In the opinion of economics scholars, this action saved the country from a financial panic and began the process of shifting the world's economic power from Europe to the United States. But it is asking Mary Pickford, Douglas Fairbanks, and Charlie Chaplin to be the spokespeople for the Third Liberty Bond tour for which he is probably best remembered.

In April 1918, one year to the day after the United States entered World War One, Secretary McAdoo's Third Liberty Loan Drive was launched to great fanfare. Leaflets were dropped from airplanes over cities and there were patriotic parades down Main Streets across the country, but ground zero for the program was Washington, D.C., where Mary Pickford, Douglas Fairbanks, Charlie Chaplin, and Broadway actress Marie Dressler were the main attraction. And while the circumstances that had brought the four to the nation's capital were solemn and serious, the actors clearly enjoyed themselves. Mary Pickford and Douglas Fairbanks arrived in good spirits; the couple got the rare opportunity to openly travel together by train on the trip across the country. But the good spirits were shared by the entire quartet of showbiz folks. In her autobiography, Mary Pickford writes about the chagrin she endured when Marie Dressler told President Woodrow Wilson an off-color joke; Mary wished "the parquet floor of the Blue Room would open up and swallow me."[7] The hijinks continued on the steps of the Treasury Department, where Charlie Chaplin got uncharacteristically carried away with emotion (in the highly charged atmosphere of the time, not to mention the parts of the Espionage Act that equated antiwar sentiments with being pro-German, Chaplin took care to keep his pacifism under wraps), took a misstep, and collided with Marie Dressler, causing both to fall on Secretary of the Navy Franklin Delano Roosevelt.

Years later, FDR would provide Mary Pickford with a photograph of that day in Washington, D.C., that she included in her autobiography, *Sunshine and Shadow*. It's a very telling picture: The politicians and military men, with FDR on the far left, are grouped around the actors and actresses in the center. Mary is holding a huge bouquet of flowers and is caught by the camera gazing adoringly at Douglas Fairbanks, who is looking straight ahead. Mary's mother, Charlotte, who had accompanied her daughter on the train ride from Los Angeles as a chaperone in an effort to quell the rumors of the couple's goings-on, is looking at the couple with a less-than-pleased expression on her face.

After meeting with the Washington bigwigs, each of the four stars went to his or her separate booth to address the crowd, sell bonds, and sign autographs. In a foreshadowing of what would happen to Pickford on her honeymoon in England more than two years later, on the way to her station she was mobbed by hordes of fans. It took her over an hour to get through the throng. It had certainly been worth it to the Treasury Department, though—the Washington, D.C., kickoff to the Liberty Bond Drive brought in more than $3 million, just under $49 million in 2017 dollars. Following their Washington, D.C., success, the quartet of actors charged with helping the Liberty Bond effort fanned out across the country. Pickford, Fairbanks, and Chaplin made their next appearance together in midtown Manhattan. After that, while the trio stayed another few days in New York, they did not appear together again. The day following the midtown appearance, Fairbanks and Chaplin, who were best friends, spoke on Wall Street to crowds estimated at fifty thousand. Three days later Mary Pickford went to the same location. Standing in front of George Washington's statue in New York City's financial district in a howling hailstorm that blew her hat off and played havoc with her famous curls, she addressed crowds massed along Broadway, Wall, Broad, and Nassau streets. Shouting against the wind as the crowds surged toward her to hear what she was saying, Pickford exhorted the crowds to buy bonds, saying, "Every bond you buy is a nail in the Kaiser's coffin!"[8] The effort was clearly worth it because the sale was hugely successful.

And so it went for Pickford and Fairbanks and Chaplin. While Doug and Charlie did well in the Midwest and South, respectively, often addressing crowds in the tens of thousands, Mary handily outsold them. In one hour in Chicago, she sold $2 million worth of bonds, approximately $32.5 million in 2017 dollars (the total included $15,000 for one of her curls, which she auctioned). In Pittsburgh, it's reported that Mary's bond sales were $5 million, which would be more than $81 million in 2017 dollars. Judging by her autobiography, Pickford was well aware of the impact of her efforts. She acknowledged the accomplishment in Pittsburgh, but it was in the wake of a marathon-selling session in Baltimore, working from nine o'clock in the morning until midnight in what she termed "the most arduous if not the most productive day of all," that it began to dawn on Pickford that it was her presence that was fueling the sales.[9] "I sold only $450,000 in bonds, but they were almost entirely in small denominations of fifty and one hundred dollars."[10] People from all walks of life, including those who could only afford bonds in the smaller denominations, listened to her and acted on what she said.

Across the country the press went crazy. From the moment the train, dubbed "The Three Star Special," left Los Angeles on April 1, 1918, with the trio of film stars (and Charlotte Pickford) aboard on its way to Washington, until the tour wrapped up weeks later, there were front-page stories preceding their arrival and extensive coverage of the events, complete with multiple photographs and follow-up articles on the results of the rallies. And it's easy to understand why the press couldn't get enough: It was a twofer—positive reporting on the war effort wrapped up in celebrity coverage.

In the end, the Liberty Bond tour was an enormous success for the government, but it came with high costs for the stars who made it happen. For one, the tour was exhausting. All three of them had been working up until the moment they boarded the train in Los Angeles. (Chaplin had reportedly been up for more than two days editing *A Dog's Life*.) Before they reached Washington, at each of the train's whistle-stops, one of the three would address the crowds that had gathered at the station. There were also legal tangles lying in wait: As soon as each of the three stars arrived in New York, they were served with lawsuits. Pickford's was from a woman who wanted a commission for purportedly helping her secure a contract; Chaplin was served by his previous studio, Essanay, for moving to Mutual; and Fairbanks was sued by Scribner's Publishing, who claimed that his movie *The Americano* was based on *The White Mice*, by Richard Harding Davis, and not *Blaze Derringer*.[11] There might not have been anything unusual in this— lawsuits were becoming an ever more frequent companion to the stars' success and were immediately handed over to the lawyers—but they were annoying nevertheless.

For Douglas Fairbanks' wife Beth, though, the over-whelming publicity the tour generated, specifically about Doug and Mary traveling together, was the breaking point for her marriage. Douglas' actions didn't help much, either. According to biographies of Douglas Fairbanks, supported by the actions he took, the actor preferred obfuscation to confrontation. Late in 1917, Fairbanks and his wife exchanged telegrams through which he denied that he was having an affair. There had been no official separation, but by 1918 Beth and Douglas Jr. were living in New York City at the Algonquin Hotel, ostensibly so the boy could go to school. However, the situation reached critical mass when Fairbanks arrived in New York from the Washington, D.C., rally. Instead of going to the Algonquin, where his wife and son were waiting for him, he checked in to the Hotel New Netherland, the prede-cessor to the Sherry Netherland Hotel. Eventually Douglas did go over to the Algonquin. He had two pur-poses in mind: to pick up his son to accompany him to the rally on Wall Street, and to confess to Beth that he and Mary Pickford were in love.[12] When Douglas left New York to continue on the Liberty Bond tour, Beth spoke to the press, announcing her separation from her husband, confirming that Douglas had confessed that he had fallen in love with someone else and that all the rumors had a basis in fact. It's worth noting two things, though: In the published interview Mary Pickford's name is not mentioned, and Beth said there would not be a divorce. Suddenly the press had two agendas when it came to Fairbanks: covering his participation on the Liberty Bond tour and relentlessly asking questions about his marriage. After initially claiming the news about the separation from his wife was pro-German propaganda, Fairbanks became frenetic, visiting as many locations as possible with a seemingly inexhaustible press corps on his heels. By the middle of April, Fairbanks, who usually couldn't get enough attention from the press, was unable to stand the combined stress of the Liberty Bond tour and the scrutiny of his personal life anymore. He had reason to be worried. There was nothing new about marital infidelity, but no one knew what the ramifications of a highly publicized breakup would be for Douglas Fairbanks' movie career, which was, after all, only two years old. Conventional wisdom of the era decreed that infidelity followed by a divorce would be a death knell to his career. In mid-April, Fairbanks canceled the balance of his tour and returned home to Los Angeles. By May, Fairbanks was back at work. He worked throughout the rest of the spring and summer of 1918 on films that supported the war effort. For a man who lived to be in the limelight, that spring and summer Fairbanks did a remarkable job keeping a low profile, only emerging for in-person appearances in support of the war. Even when Mary Pickford joined the rest of the Hollywood power elite to found the Motion Picture Relief Organization in June 1918, Fairbanks passed on attending the inaugural meeting, sending a telegram with his regrets. The organization elected him vice president in spite of his absence.[13] Fairbanks also found new digs, leasing Silsby Spalding's fifteen-acre estate in Beverly Hills. According to those who were working with him at the time, Fairbanks was back to his happy and outgoing self by midsummer.

In fact, Fairbanks was as popular as ever, especially with the soldiers overseas who were being entertained by his films. The press blowup that had accompanied the end of his marriage had been mercifully brief and was in the rearview mirror; Fairbanks emerged from the ordeal with his career intact. Considering how important Douglas Fairbanks and Mary Pickford were to the war effort, it's entirely possible that George Creel's CPI exerted pressure on the press to tread lightly.[14] Fairbanks and Pickford, often in disguise, continued their relationship. Keeping the affair under wraps was probably helped along by Creel's

CPI leaning on news outlets as well as Charlotte Pickford's prowess bribing witnesses who threatened to expose the lovers.

After Beth Fairbanks' interview with the press was published, the Liberty Bond tour was no picnic for Mary Pickford, either. Unlike Doug, though, she completed her schedule of stops throughout the Northeast before returning to Los Angeles. Owen Moore, Pickford's husband with whom she hadn't lived for years, started to make rumblings. There were rumors that Moore was going to sue and that he had threatened to shoot Fairbanks. To Mary it didn't matter what her husband said, or said he was going to do; it was all nonsense, and she abhorred negative publicity. When Pickford was asked for a quote following Beth's interview, she prevaricated, saying she had no idea why her name was being mentioned in a matter between husband and wife. After she had returned to Los Angeles and was preparing to go back to work at the studio, she was asked if she planned to retire from making movies. Pickford's reply was directly on point. She admonished the press to look over the studio's fence the following morning and there they would see her working. Follow-up questions on the subject were not encouraged. As added insurance, *Photoplay* magazine was invited into Mary and Owen's home for an "Our Mary and Her Owen" photo shoot of the stars at home.

Beth Fairbanks had taken the reins of the financial side of her nonconfrontational husband's career, but Pickford, who was hands-on in the negotiations of her own studio contracts, had little doubt of their financial clout in their industry. In spite of the fact that Pickford had no formal training in business— indeed, she had very little formal schooling at all— from the beginning of her career at the age of five years, she quickly developed a keen sense of her worth to her employers. More importantly, once she determined her worth, she was able to communicate the remuneration to which she thought she was entitled. In the autobiographical articles and books she wrote over the years, she often proclaimed that she strove constantly for more money because she figured every year in the entertainment business would be her last. Mary Pickford knew she and Douglas Fairbanks were rich, she knew they were famous; what she learned from addressing crowds across the country during the Liberty Bond tour was that she and Doug were influential far beyond the world of moviemaking. And being the astute student of life experiences that she was, she would remember this like she remembered all of her lessons. The combined experience of being on tour to support the war and encourage the purchase of Liberty Bonds and having their personal lives discussed openly in the press had to have been profoundly instructive to Pickford and Fairbanks. What Mary also learned was that money, fame, and influence could not guarantee privacy; however, assistance from a sympathetic government could. The mechanics of avoiding unwanted scrutiny was still a work in process.

5

Veni, Vidi, Vici

———◇◇———

Douglas Fairbanks was the first of the "picture folk" to set up housekeeping in the young city of Beverly Hills. His first home was Grayhall, Silsby Spalding's estate, which he rented in 1918. It was indeed a house for a star: situated on fifteen acres of prime land that included tennis courts, an outdoor pool, stables, dog kennels and a view of the Pacific Ocean.[1] Fairbanks settled right in to the house and the neighborhood. He filmed parts of *He Comes Up Smiling*, written by Frances Marion, on location at the home. In an early indication of his civic commitment to the city, after the volunteer Beverly Hills Fire Department doused the flames of a fire that broke out in a living room chimney at Grayhall (which resulted in $20,000 in losses, including the damage to and destruction of several Frederic Remington paintings from Fairbanks' budding collection of the Western artist's works), Fairbanks treated the firemen to dinner in another room of the estate.[2]

Because he had landed in such grand digs, it might seem a bit counterintuitive that Fairbanks was in the market for something else in the neighborhood, something secluded. It was Stanley Anderson of the Beverly Hills Hotel who, in 1919, pointed Fairbanks to a rustic six-room hunting lodge north of the hotel on Summit Drive that lacked both running water and electricity. Fairbanks bought the house overlooking the Beverly Hills Hotel for $35,000. While it's true Fairbanks had a grander plan for the eighteen acres that surrounded the small structure, initially the lodge served the purpose of a secluded hideaway for the star.

The point wasn't necessarily to move his official domicile—at least not yet. He was looking for a remote, private spot out of the public eye where he could woo his paramour. Remote and private being the operative objectives because Douglas Fairbanks needed to keep his affair with Mary Pickford, the most famous woman in the world, who happened to be married to someone else, a secret.

Douglas Fairbanks had come a long way, literally and figuratively, on the journey to Beverly Hills, California. He was born Douglas Elton Thomas Ullman on May 23, 1883, in Denver, Colorado. His father, Charles Ullman, was the son of German Jewish immigrants who had settled in Pennsylvania. His mother, Ella March, was a Catholic Southern belle. Both of Fairbanks' parents had been married multiple times, not necessarily waiting until the previous marriage had been legally terminated before embarking on their next set of nuptials. In fact, it's possible that Charles Ullman's previous marriage had not been legally terminated when he wed Ella. Ella herself had been married twice before marrying Ullman. Her first husband, John Fairbanks Sr., had died and her second, Edward Wilcox, was an alcoholic whom she divorced. Charles Ullman had been her lawyer. Eventually Ullman discovered that Ella had a wandering eye and, when confronted with his wife's adultery, left her and their two sons, Douglas and Robert. Ella retaliated by assuming the last name of her first husband, by whom she also had a son, John Fairbanks Jr., for the entire family.

By all accounts, Douglas Fairbanks had been a showoff and a ham from childhood. He took to acting early in amateur and summer stock in the Denver area. By the time he was in high school, where he was once suspended for putting costumes on the campus statues, he was in demand as an actor in the area. In

1900, before completing his senior year of high school, he left Denver as part of a traveling acting troupe bound for New York and a life on the stage. He never finished high school and did not, as he is reported to have claimed, attend the Colorado School of Mines, Harvard, or Princeton. After arriving in New York, Doug worked in a hardware store and as a clerk on Wall Street while waiting for his break on Broadway, which came in 1902. He rose to fame on the boards. In 1907, Douglas Fairbanks married Beth Sully, the daughter of a wealthy businessman. By 1915, the year he met Mary Pickford in New York, Doug was working in Los Angeles for D. W. Griffith. The physicality of his performance was not to Griffith's taste, but it caught the attention of Anita Loos and John Emerson, respectively the young industry's top screenwriter and director. The pair would go on to write and direct many of Doug's signature romantic comedies over the next few years.

If Douglas Fairbanks began his life in straitened circumstances, Mary Pickford—born Gladys Louise Smith in Toronto, Ontario, on April 8, 1892—marked her early years with increasing degrees of poverty. Also of mixed religious background—her father, John Smith, was the son of a Methodist minister and her mother, Charlotte Hennessey, was a Catholic of Irish descent—Mary's early life was full of death, disease, and despair. Her father yo-yoed in and out of the family home and, when Mary was six, died of a head injury sustained at his job with Niagara Steamship. After her husband's death Charlotte worked in a grocery store during the day and took in sewing at night. Frequently the family's neighbors provided food for the young brood, which included Mary's younger sister and brother, Lottie and Jack. At one point Charlotte contemplated letting a wealthy doctor and his wife adopt Mary. But after a visit to the couple's luxurious home, where Mary learned that the offer of adoption was for her alone and didn't include her brother and sister, she adamantly refused. By some accounts it was then that Mary felt the full burden of responsibility for her family.[3] She didn't quite know how she would accomplish it, but she was determined to take care of her mother and siblings.

Her introduction to acting came via the stage manager of a theater company, whom Charlotte Smith had taken in as a boarder. He suggested that the two sisters, Mary and Lottie, appear in the company's next production, which debuted on January 8, 1900. After eight performances, the girls each earned $10, which they gave to their mother. A star—and a stage mother—was born.

By 1906, after performing with touring stock companies throughout the United States, traveling by rail and staying in cramped rooming houses along the way, Mary Pickford and her family landed in New York. It was there, when she appeared in a supporting role in a play written by William C. deMille, brother of Cecil B., that the play's producer, David Belasco, insisted Gladys Smith create a stage name. They settled on Mary Pickford, cobbled together from Marie, the middle name she had been given when Charlotte had her baptized as a Catholic when Mary was sick with diphtheria in 1896, and the middle name of Charlotte's father, John Pickford Hennessey. Charlotte kenned quickly that Mary was destined for big things: The entire family changed their last name to Pickford. In May 1909, Mary did a screen test for D. W. Griffith at the Biograph Company and by the end of the same year had done fifty-one films, mostly one-reelers, for them. She reasoned that if she worked hard, performed often, and appeared in as many films as she could, she would create a demand for her work. It was an excellent plan. In fact, considering Mary was just seventeen at the time she made it, it was an extremely well-thought-out plan. In short order, Mary Pickford had negotiated a rate of $10 a day with a $40 weekly guarantee from Biograph. In January 1910, Mary traveled to California to shoot more films. In those early days, film actors went unbilled. Mary Pickford was known as "The Girl with the Golden Curls" and "The Biograph Girl." She returned briefly to the Broadway stage in 1912, but found that she missed working in film. By 1913, she had returned exclusively to making movies. All along the way, with every change of studio, Mary banked on her fame and ability to draw audiences when she negotiated deals with producers, the frameworks of which were not only models for other actors of the era, but are still in use to this day (guaranteed salaries with a percentage of the gross). By the middle of the second decade of the twentieth century, Mary Pickford was among the highest-paid—by some accounts, the highest-paid—actor working in film.

She married the handsome Irish actor Owen Moore in early 1911, against her mother's wishes. By all accounts, Charlotte's instincts about Moore were on target: He was an abusive alcoholic and jealous of his wife's growing fame and his lack thereof. At the end of their marriage, Mary would settle with Moore for $100,000, a fortune for the time.[4]

Although they had certainly known of each other through their work—Mary had seen Doug on Broadway in 1912 with a group of fellow Biograph Company actors—Mary Pickford and Douglas Fairbanks didn't actually meet until November 1915 at a party in Tarrytown, New York, thrown by a mutual friend, Elsie Janis.

Both were there with their respective spouses, Doug with his wife Beth and Mary with Owen Moore. During the afternoon the two couples took a walk with their hostess through the late autumn chill. Jokes were made about women's shoes being ruined, but the two wives soldiered on. Beth eventually turned back, but Mary persevered. Then, while crossing a log over a frigid stream, Mary lost her nerve and froze. It was Douglas Fairbanks to the rescue when he literally swept her off her feet and carried her to solid ground.[5]

It was a rare loss of composure for Mary Pickford. She was known for roles as a determined, plucky young woman who used her wits to turn often insurmountable obstacles to her advantage. And to a great extent, that's exactly who she was: Mary Pickford had been responsible for supporting her sister, brother, and mother for so long she probably couldn't remember a time when that hadn't been the case. By the time she met Doug Fairbanks, she was in a deeply unhappy marriage to Moore, who is described as "an insecure, bitter, evidently unlikable, handsome drunk" by Tracey Goessel in *The First King of Hollywood*, her excellent biography of Douglas Fairbanks.

Doug Fairbanks was by all accounts an athletic,

good-looking, good-natured, fun-loving, charming lady's man who didn't drink to excess and didn't gamble. Through the years he had been linked to actresses in a series of affairs. However, it was clear from the very start that Mary Pickford was not going to be a casual fling. After Doug arranged a few, completely proper, meetings that included Doug introducing Mary to his mother, Ella, as well as meeting Mary's mother, Charlotte, the two went their separate ways, back to their flourishing careers as the biggest movie stars of the time. Mary was temporarily in New York making movies for Paramount and Doug went back to California with its more clement weather to shoot films. His work ranged from playing "Coke Ennyday," the cocaine-addicted detective based on Sherlock Holmes, in the zany comedy whose display advertising described the movie as the "1916 Cocaine Classic from the folks who brought you *Reefer Madness*," *The Mystery of the Leaping Fish*, to *The Half Breed*, one of the most serious films in his oeuvre.

Mary and Doug met up again in the summer of 1916 when Doug took the starring role in *Manhattan Madness*. Conjecture has it that one of the motivating factors for his return to New York was proximity to Mary, who was living at the time in Larchmont.[6]

Biographers and historians believe that their physical relationship began after the death of Doug's mother

in late 1916; at least that was when the passionate letters from Doug to Mary started. But secrecy, especially
for Mary, was paramount. Mary Pickford took her
reputation in the popular press seriously—to the
point where she "penned" a daily column describing
her thoughts and observations that was syndicated
and appeared in newspapers across the country.
(The columns were in fact ghostwritten, many by pi-
oneering screenwriter and frequent Mary Pickford
collaborator Frances Marion.) The double standard
of what men and women could get away with in their
private lives was very much in force. If word got out
that she was a loose woman, not to mention an un-
faithful wife, Mary did not believe that being the
most famous woman in the world would protect her
from the blowback. In light of the public's reaction to
the series of scandals that would plague fellow actors
in the near future, her instincts were spot-on. Mary
knew that adverse publicity of any magnitude would
hit her in her most sensitive spot: her pocketbook.
There are stories of Charlotte Pickford chasing Doug
from Mary's dressing room with a gun and of hiring
publicists to pay off any witnesses to the couple's special
friendship.

After the wildly successful 1918 Liberty Bond
tour, Mary returned to Los Angeles more or less per-
manently. To maintain secrecy, the couple donned

disguises and sneaked around town. They sometimes met at Doug's brother Robert's house. And for all anyone knows—because part of its allure from the very beginning was discretion—they may have also met at the Beverly Hills Hotel.

Mary Pickford was all about her work. She had been at it so long, and had been so successful, that work for her was no longer second nature; it was her purpose. From the very beginning at the theater in Toronto when, as a child of six or seven, she asked for bigger parts and more money, to becoming one of the first actors to form a production company, to teaming up with fellow industry talent to form United Artists in order to maximize their revenue from their films by controlling distribution, Mary was always driven. America's Sweetheart may have looked like innocence personified, but underneath those blond curls was one of the most astute brains to ever work in the motion picture industry. Mary understood the power of the press and its ability to manipulate public opinion; she for one had utilized it when she took her battle for a fatter paycheck to the broadsheets. The reproving oversight of the studios was a fact of life for her—she was beginning to play roles as children such as *Pollyanna* and *Rebecca of Sunnybrook Farm*. But Mary didn't have a problem with this. She was in the illusion business and understood perception; Mary was not going to do anything to jeopardize her bankability.

Ultimately Doug's hunting lodge on Summit Drive solved the problem of ensuring the couple's privacy before Mary's divorce and their marriage. The humble six-room lodge that would eventually evolve into Pickfair marked the beginning of a beautiful, permanent friendship between a city and its famous residents.

On March 2, 1920, Mary Pickford divorced Owen Moore in Reno, Nevada. On March 28, 1920, she married Douglas Fairbanks. Six weeks later the couple left for their honeymoon. The trip would hold more than a few revelations for the newlyweds. Their Liberty Bond tour in 1918 proved they were popular. This trip would prove that the public's reaction to the couple's fame transcended popularity with a sort of grand hysteria that was something altogether different. Douglas Fairbanks and Mary Pickford's fame had gone global in a way that was completely new. There had never been anything quite like the pandemonium they caused wherever they went. As they traveled across the continent to New York to catch the boat to England, their train was swamped. Thousands waited to greet them in New York and see them off; thousands greeted them when the ship docked at Southampton. Fairbanks would have to extricate his terrified bride from the throngs that reached into the open cars in which they traveled to touch America's Sweetheart. In one instance, Fairbanks had to place Mary on his shoulders to separate her from the adoring-yet-crushing crowd. English fans almost loved Mary to death.

But the couple soon discovered that lack of recognition was just as disturbing in its own way as an overabundance of attention. Douglas and Mary thought it might be nice to seek out some quiet alone time, so while they were in Holland, the pair drove to Germany, where their films had not been shown during World War One. According to a recollection of the trip by Mary, during a day of shopping and sightseeing, the couple did not see a flicker of recognition on the faces of any of the people they encountered. When Fairbanks asked if she liked being left alone, Mary responded that she "definitely" did not and wanted to go back to where they were known. After one day she had "had enough obscurity for a lifetime."

After that brief interlude of anonymity in Germany, the world for Douglas and Mary returned to spinning the right way and the couple were met with adoring crowds throughout the rest of their European tour, which included stops in Switzerland, Italy, and France.

But it was the return to New York that was unlike anything anyone had ever seen before. Having heard about the couple's reception in England, American fans, who felt ownership of the pair and would not be outdone in over-the-top adoration, pulled out all the stops. There were competing bands set up on platforms to greet the ship when it docked on the west side of Manhattan and a police motorcycle escort through a phalanx of fans lining the route to the couple's hotel on Fifth Avenue.

When Mary and Douglas returned home from their honeymoon late in the summer of 1920, Beverly Hills would provide a respite not just from what their lives had been, but also from what they had become.

And the home to which they returned, Pickfair, was something to behold. The house was designed by Wallace Neff, California's first homegrown star-chitect. In no way a provincial, Neff came from an extremely wealthy family; he was the grandson of Chicago printing tycoon Andrew McNally (of Rand McNally fame), who had moved to Southern California to found Rancho La Mirada with Neff's father, Edwin. When he was nine, Neff moved to Europe with his family, returning to the United States in 1916 at age nineteen when war broke out. While Neff is credited with developing the "California style," a mash-up of Spanish Colonial Revival and Mission with touches of Tudor and Gothic, his education was with Ralph Adams Cram, the revered New England–based architect who specialized in collegiate and ecclesiastical buildings designed in Gothic Revival style.

The mock-Tudor mansion that Neff devised was perched at the top of a hill, surrounded by eighteen landscaped acres, complete with stables, an in-ground swimming pool large enough for Doug and Mary to paddle around it in a canoe, tennis courts, servants' quarters, automobile garages, and a guest wing. Inside it had frescoed ceilings, parquet wood floors, rooms and hallways paneled in mahogany and bleached pine as well as decorative niches embellished with gold leaf and mirrors. There was an Old West saloon complete with an ornate burnished mahogany bar. Even though Doug almost always abstained from alcohol, the saloon made a great setting for his collection of Frederic Remington paintings and sculptures.

Pickfair was meant to be a palace and was described accordingly. The house was dubbed by *Life* magazine as "a gathering place only slightly less important than the White House . . . and much more fun," which is probably a statement that's more fancy than fact. In truth, while an invitation to Pickfair was coveted—receiving one meant that you had "arrived"—the idea of visiting could be much more fulfilling than the actual event. Contemporaries of Doug and Mary were effusive in their descriptions of the house, its interiors, and the fetes that took place there. In a 1980 interview with Kevin Brownlow recorded for the documentary TV series *Hollywood*, Lord Louis Mountbatten recalled that Pickfair was "certainly, the most, best taste house, I should think, in Hollywood, and run very much on English country house lines. . . . It was like Buckingham Palace; it was the house that everyone wanted to go to. . . ."[7] But behind the dramatic mock-Tudor exterior walls of Pickfair, much of the furnishing was prosaic and pedestrian, and the parties dull and dry, as in little to no alcohol was served. Although there were antiques scattered throughout the house, most of the furniture was "solid department-store copies of European styles such as Babbitt himself might use to adorn his new house in the Midwest."[8] The dinner parties, at which no wine was served, ended promptly at ten so Doug and Mary could go to bed in order to get up early the following morning and go to work. Two conclusions could be drawn from these descriptions: that, in spite of the grandeur in which they surrounded themselves, Doug and Mary were at heart parvenus; or the couple—who were very aware of how they were perceived by the public and whose lives were lived very much in a fishbowl—chose their furnishings and adopted an entertaining style as a calculated decision to remain well within the accepted norms of middle-American values, "a way of not moving too conspicuously beyond the taste of the millions of fans who also bought their furniture at department stores and went to bed early on week nights so as to be at work the next morning on time. . . ."[9]

The carpets, sofas, tables, and chairs may have reflected the tastes of their millions of less well-heeled fans, but Doug and Mary set themselves up in style. Each had their own suite of rooms: Doug's included a bedroom, bathroom, a walk-in closet large enough to house his extensive wardrobe, a hall, and, because this was before the advent of air-conditioning, a screened-in sleeping porch. Mary's suite is described as being painted lavender with dull green furniture. In addition to her bedroom, she also had her own bathroom and a sleeping porch. After his morning exercises, Fairbanks chose what he would wear that day from "fifty pairs of shoes, thousand shirts, seventy suits, thirty-five coats and thirty-seven hats."[10] At six, Mary and Doug met in the ivory-colored breakfast room to sip tea from a silver service and plan their respective days.

It wasn't the furnishings, quotidian or not, that set Pickfair aside, it was the people who crossed the threshold. Charlie Chaplin was at his best friend Doug's house so often, the so-called Rose Room was reserved for him. Other guests who graced their dinner table and attended screenings of not-yet-released movies included cultural royalty Greta Garbo, George Bernard Shaw, Albert Einstein, Helen Keller, H. G. Wells, Amelia Earhart, Charles Lindbergh, F. Scott Fitzgerald, Noël Coward, Pearl S. Buck, Arthur Conan Doyle, old friends Lillian and Dorothy Gish, and, to show there were no hard feelings about dodging his patent enforcements, Thomas Edison. Actual royalty were frequent guests, too, including the Duke and Duchess of Windsor, Lord Louis Mountbatten, the Duke and Duchess of Alba, and the King and Queen of Siam. Oh, and Franklin and Eleanor Roosevelt.

(Some things in industry social gatherings haven't changed much, such as screenings. Invariably, Doug would fall asleep, only to wake at the end of the film and proclaim it the best he had ever seen.)

In some ways, the grand honeymoon complete with adoring crowds in attendance was the final step in a long journey that was both literal and metaphorical for Mary and Douglas. With their triumphant return to Beverly Hills both demonstrated how far they had come: for Mary, from Toronto, through grueling years of poverty and an abusive husband, and for Doug, from Denver, possible illegitimacy and knowing he was half-Jewish—something that would haunt Fairbanks throughout his life. Mary Pickford and Douglas Fairbanks had arrived; they had transcended the cold shoulders of so-called proper society. Through their wits, determination, and talent, without much formal education or well-heeled, socially connected families, as individuals the couple had climbed to the top of the world. Now, with their honeymoon to Europe behind them, the couple returned home. And home in Beverly Hills was a safety zone where the past did not weigh on the present and where not being listed on the Social Register was immaterial. Beverly Hills was where they could bask in a place where everyone knew their names and they were the undisputed king and queen of all that they surveyed. Their marriage to each other was exponentially more than two of the world's biggest stars as husband and wife. It was the stuff of dreams and legends and it had set up shop in the young city of Beverly Hills. Douglas and Mary reigning from Pickfair became a magnet for their fellow stars and successful people of all occupations. They were the model that the stars of the new medium wished to emulate; Douglas and Mary had pioneered the path to what fame in the motion picture industry looked like and where it lived. Motion picture stars did not have to chase their public; the world, including presidents, kings, queens, princes; and princesses, would flock to them.

It's possible that had Douglas Fairbanks not been the first star to decamp to Beverly Hills, the migration might have shaped up much differently. Doug was larger than life in almost every way; he was both a natural leader and organizer *and* a tastemaker. If Doug Fairbanks was doing something, if he had either joined or founded an organization, wore his hair a particular way, drove a certain car, or moved west to a new city, it struck those who knew him as the right thing to do. And not only did he move to Beverly Hills, he brought Mary Pickford with him. About that same time Charlie Chaplin, who along with Fairbanks and Pickford was one of the world's biggest stars, also moved to Beverly Hills. After Fairbanks, Pickford, and Chaplin, a tsunami of movie stars, directors, screenwriters, and producers followed, including Gloria Swanson, Tom Mix, Carl Laemmle, Ronald Colman, John Barrymore, Buster Keaton, Harold Lloyd, Fred Niblo, Will Rogers, Jack Warner, Clara Bow, Rudolph Valentino, and the Gish sisters. Everyone wanted to be as close as they could be to the gods of the motion picture industry, and their Mount Olympus was undisputedly where Douglas Fairbanks and Mary Pickford lived: Pickfair in Beverly Hills.

Beverly Hills was no longer a faraway whistle-stop on Henry Huntington's Dinky line. As of late 1920, it was now the center of the universe.

6

The War Against Hollywood and the Lasting Legacy of Bad Behavior

——◇◇◇——

World War One had forged an inexorable link between the federal government and the emerging motion picture industry. The experience of the partnership during the war had taught a few important lessons to Hollywood's emerging power elite, especially Adolph Zukor, Mary Pickford, and Douglas Fairbanks, chiefly that there was a potential for reciprocity. Mary and Doug had shown that their celebrity quotient had been the secret sauce in a successful Liberty Bond campaign; Adolph Zukor and his fellow studio, distribution, and exhibitor executives had proved themselves an invaluable resource in creating targeted content. Or, in other words, with the right incentive they would jump on the propaganda bandwagon. Certain government officials had been quick to see the advantage of enlisting these newfangled celebrities and the movie business executives in selling causes and raising money.

In spite of the fact that Hollywood and the Democratic administration of Woodrow Wilson, especially Treasury Secretary William McAdoo, had a fruitful and successful partnership during World War One, in the 1920 presidential elections Hollywood's power players looked at the field and decided that the Republican candidate, Warren G. Harding, was their man. Zukor had received assurances that Harding's administration wouldn't interfere with the moviemaker's business practices. Now, Harding is almost always named as one of the worst presidents of all time, his name inexorably linked to the suitcases of cash that changed hands between oilmen and government officials for leases on oil reserves during the Teapot Dome Scandal (which had its own Beverly Hills connection through oilman Edward Doheny, who provided one of those self-same suitcases). However, at the time of his nomination, Harding presented himself as pro-business, anti-organized labor, anti-Bolshevik, and an advocate of lower personal income taxes who was keenly interested in new technologies like automobiles, aviation, radio, and motion pictures. What's perhaps most telling of all is that Harding appointed the Republican National Committee chairman Will Hayes to a succession of government posts, before Hayes was lured by the motion picture industry chieftains to be their handpicked censor in chief. Hayes knew the players in Hollywood and, more importantly for the studio honchos, they knew him.

Like everything else, Hollywood and the business of making movies was changing, though. Back in 1910 when D. W. Griffith and Mary Pickford had first traveled to Hollywood to make movies in the February sunshine, filmmaking was still new enough that there was an air of adventure about the whole enterprise. Making a moving picture in 1910 really was the equivalent of kids putting on a show; by 1920 the kids who had been putting on those shows had evolved into corporations. The movie business had matured into an industry with its companies listed on the New York Stock Exchange. Government scrutiny had become a cost of doing business. Men such as Adolph Zukor had set up their studios as vertical monopolies; they controlled the entire pipeline for the movies the public consumed, from hiring writers and actors to filming to distribution and exhibition. It was exactly the sort of monopoly that "trustbusters" on the Federal Trade Commission, which had been established in 1915 by the administration of President Wilson primarily to

break up railroad monopolies, were seeking to elimi-
nate. For the movie business in the early 1920s, the
stakes were high; real money was involved. Zukor and
his fellow studio chiefs depended on Harding to keep
the regulators' eyes focused anywhere but on the
motion picture industry.

But it wasn't just the scrutiny of federal government
agencies that the moviemakers wanted to dodge. With
each passing year it seemed there were more and more
civilian organizations howling for the right to censor films.

Once the Volstead Act had passed in 1919 outlawing the sale and consumption of alcohol, those who
had what California historian Kevin Starr termed
"fundamentalist rectitude,"[1] the kind that populated
the Christian Temperance Union and other like-
minded organizations, turned their attention to
cleaning up the rest of the moral morass into which
they felt the United States was devolving. This battle,
for no less than the souls of the country according to
those who were taking up figurative arms, pitted
newly minted Hollywood moguls, like Adolph Zukor[2]
and Jesse Lasky, along with the actors and actresses in
front of the cameras, against the decency brigade of
church ladies (and gentlemen) who felt that the movies were just another example, like alcohol, of the
perfidy and moral corruption that was destroying

America. For Zukor and other producers and exhibitors, it was no less than a war on two fronts: deflecting the growing interest of the Department of Justice in the vertical integration of studios, which made movies and also owned the theaters that exhibited them, and keeping the ever-growing numbers of censors from exacting control over the movies' content.

The late teens and early twenties was a strange time. Running concurrently to optimism and high spirits that followed the end of the War to End All Wars and ushered in the Roaring Twenties, there was a groundswell of righteous indignation on the part of a self-appointed morals police to rid society of base influences like sex, drugs, alcohol, jazz—all debasements, they believed, encouraged by movies. True believers and sanctimonious hypocrites alike decried the outsize influence movies had on the young and impressionable. It was a roiling time of progressive and regressive changes coming along practically hand in hand. Hard on the heels of the ratification of the Nineteenth Amendment to the Constitution, which gave women the right to vote in national elections, had come the Twentieth Amendment outlawing alcohol, a law that enjoyed a great deal of support from women. Reactionary forces were doing their best to hang on to the last vestiges of the Victorian era's suf-

focating propriety, while new technologies like projectors and Victrolas were delivering entertainment
like movies and music, often jazz, to the masses.
Committees were formed to sit in judgment on the
wholesomeness of movie content. Unlike the pressure
the Committee for Public Information, which had
been disbanded in 1918 at the end of the war, brought
on the film community to create content that supported the war effort, this was censorship plain and
simple masquerading as "protection." In a way it was
a manifestation of the question posed in one of the
songs popular during the war about getting the young
men who had experienced European city life and culture to settle back down to their prosaic lives. "How ya
gonna keep 'em down on the farm after they've seen
Paree' / How ya gonna keep 'em away from Broadway, jazzin' around and paintin' the town."[3] The fact
was, no one could, but nothing was going to stop the
country's reactionary forces from trying.

Every city, it seemed, had at least one committee in
place to review the content of films and judge their ap-
propriateness. It was a maddening situation for the
film distributors. Something that was acceptable in
San Francisco could be anathema in Pittsburgh. Even
in one city, something that would pass muster by one
committee would be shot down by the other. Film

releases could be held up for indeterminate amounts of time.

In spite of the work Hollywood's War Cooperating Committee, which included William Fox, D. W. Griffith, Thomas H. Ince, Jesse L. Lasky, Carl Laemmle, Marcus Loew, Joseph M. Schenck, Lewis J. Selznick, and Adolph Zukor, had done during the war to help the government, the fact that most of the men who ran the movie studios were Jewish did not help their cause. Even though a strong case could be made that much of the public's idea of the American Dream was developed through movies made by the same Jews who now ran the studios, anti-Semitism was rampant and systemic. Their Jewishness was but one more reason the various decency committees cast a gimlet eye on movies coming out of Hollywood. The Jews who invented Hollywood may have embraced and extolled the American Dream, sharing their starry-eyed vision with their fellow citizens, but much of Christian America did not return the favor by accepting them as anything approaching equal. The question that roared from pulpits from coast to coast was how could Jews possibly uphold Christian morals? And nothing could bridge that religious divide, including Adolph Zukor having the largest Christmas tree in town.

Then there were the actors and actresses themselves. It was a nightmare scenario for those filled with fundamentalist rectitude: beautiful and restless young men and women (mostly women, it seemed) descending on Hollywood, unfettered by supervision, with hopes for fame, fortune, and adventure fueled by the proliferation of movie magazines. Morality Leagues, churches, Women's Clubs, and other organizations viewed the young people pouring into Hollywood as sybarites who were setting a bad example for the rest of the youth of America, plain and simple. And, to a great extent, the new arrivals in Hollywood did little to help their own cause in the eyes of the morals' monitors. They partied often and they partied hard.

The actual town of Hollywood had changed. In 1910, when Mary Pickford first came west to make movies, the teetotaler city, which was still mostly orchards, had just voted to annex itself to Los Angeles. By 1920, when Mary moved to Beverly Hills from the Craftsman bungalow in Hollywood that she shared with her mother (rather than her husband Owen Moore), the population had skyrocketed. Between 1910 and 1920 the population of Los Angeles nearly doubled, from 319,198 to 576,673, fueled in part by the growth of the movie industry. According to the 1910 census there were about 400 actors and just north of 200 actresses; by 1920 the number of actors and actresses had multiplied almost sixfold to 2,300 and 1,300, respectively. In addition to talent in front of the camera there were also legions of people such as producers, directors, cameramen, lighting technicians, costumers, scenarists, carpenters, costumers, hairdressers, makeup artists, scene painters, and so on who had moved to Hollywood to work in the new industry.[4] It was a boomtown.

Even if her commute between home and studio wasn't via chauffeured cars, Mary Pickford would probably have been able to handle the crowds well enough. She had lived in New York and had taken her share of public transportation and even done her share of walking between home and work to save bus and subway fare. What she was extremely averse to was scandal. As bad as Mary may have felt about the brouhaha surrounding her divorce and her new husband's separation and divorce from his first wife, she was savvy enough to realize she had dodged a bullet. Her popularity—and even more importantly, her pocketbook—emerged from the experience intact. But instinctively she knew that bad publicity attached to a scandal could stem from little more than being in the wrong place at the wrong time. In the time between when she settled into Pickfair, which

Douglas Fairbanks had given her as a wedding gift, and the first rumblings of a proposed annexation of Beverly Hills to Los Angeles, three scandals rocked the moviemaking world. These were no ordinary tales of people behaving badly, getting caught in flagrante delicto, suing for divorce, being arrested for buying or consuming alcohol, or getting caught (or arrested) for driving drunk. The three scandals that roiled Hollywood—and the world, for that matter—were soaked in sin (alcohol, drugs, and sex) that had resulted in death, both accidental and murder.

The first of the trio of high-profile scandals to brush up against the Hollywood community may have happened almost half a world away in Paris, France, but the death by accidental poisoning—after a night of copious consumption of drugs and alcohol—of Olive Thomas, who was married to Mary Pickford's younger brother, Jack, hit close to home.

Olive Thomas, born Olive Duffy in Pennsylvania in 1894, moved to New York City in 1913 following the end of a brief marriage to Bernard Thomas. She started her show business career in 1914 at the age of twenty by winning "The Most Beautiful Girl in New York City" contest. The contest was held by renowned illustrator Howard Chandler Christy, and the winner was to become the model for what Christy dubbed "The Christy Girl." His illustrations of the Christy Girl came to replace illustrator Charles Dana Gibson's fin de siècle Gibson Girl as the romanticized archetype of American womanhood. Olive Thomas also posed for other prominent New York illustrators including Harrison Fisher, Raphael Kirchner, and Haskell Coffin. She appeared on a cover of the *Saturday Evening Post* and posed nude from the waist up for Peruvian artist Alberto Vargas before being hired for the *Ziegfeld Follies*. (There was a bit of a dispute over how she got the Ziegfeld job. According to Fisher, he wrote her a letter of recommendation to Florenz Ziegfeld; Olive Thomas claimed she approached Ziegfeld herself and asked. Such are the makings of personal legend.)

Olive is reputed to have cut a wide swath through the prominent men of the time before marrying Jack Pickford. She had an affair with Florenz Ziegfeld, which she is said to have ended when he wouldn't leave his wife at the time, Billie Burke. In 1916, Olive started her film career in a serial for International Film Company. By 1917 she had graduated to feature films—and a high-profile love interest. In the second half of 1916, Olive had met Jack Pickford and Mary Pickford at a café at the Santa Monica Pier. According to Mary's close friend and frequent collaborator, screenwriter Frances Marion, Jack and Olive were like peas in a pod when it came to a predilection for hard partying. Marion called them "the gayest, wildest brats who ever stirred the stardust on Broadway. Both were talented, but they were much more interested in playing the roulette of life than in concentrating on their careers."[5] Although Olive announced her engagement to Jack Pickford in 1917, the couple had married in October 1916 in New Jersey. Mary was not amused. In her autobiography she wrote, "I regret to say that none of us approved. Mother thought Jack was too young, and Lottie and I felt that Olive, being in musical comedy, belonged to an alien world."[6] A bit rich on Mary's part, as, at the time she married Jack, Olive had fully made the transition to movies from the *Ziegfeld Follies* and would go on to appear in a number of feature-length films, including her penultimate film in 1920, *The Flapper,* by Frances Marion, which introduced the term to the American lexicon.

It was a tumultuous union, to say the least. There were huge fights followed by excessive outpourings of affection and the presentation of costly gifts from Jack to Olive. In 1920, the couple decided to take a trip to Europe to give their marriage another chance. Their companion on the trip? None other than Mary's ex-husband Owen Moore. Talk about keeping it all in the family. The proliferation of movie mags that had sprung up to cover the young industry and its beautiful denizens followed Olive and Jack's relationship closely and covered it breathlessly.

According to the articles in newspapers, on the fateful night, the couple partied well into the early hours, imbibing champagne and, according to some accounts, ingesting huge quantities of cocaine. After returning to their hotel, Olive drank from a bottle that contained the mercury bichloride that Jack was using as a topical treatment for his chronic syphilis. Jack and Owen Moore rushed her to American Hospital, where she died five days later. The press on both sides of the Atlantic went wild with speculation that Olive had committed suicide for any number of reasons: Jack's infidelities or that Jack had infected her with syphilis. Some reports speculated that she was a hopeless drug fiend and others suggested Jack had murdered her for the insurance money. While there was no love lost between Mary and her late sister-in-law, Mary felt responsible for her wayward brother Jack's welfare. Nevertheless, each and every one of these journalistic screeds, in which her name was always mentioned, must have hit Mary like a physical blow. Adding insult to injury, the reports never failed to mention the loathsome Owen, further reminding readers that Mary was a divorced woman who was part of a family that engaged in drug-fueled goings-on and had members being treated for syphilis.

Jack Pickford brought his wife's body back for her funeral at Saint Thomas Episcopal Church in New York City on September 28, 1920. It became the first celebrity-fueled frenzy since Mary and Doug's triumphant return from their honeymoon just a few weeks earlier. The church was jammed, women fainted, and everyone was packed tight in the queue to see the casket. The media were in attack mode, struggling to recognize the celebrity contingent attending. Necks were craned to their breaking point looking for the deceased's famous sister-in-law, Mary Pickford. But Mary, along with Doug, stayed in Beverly Hills and did not attend. However, both had been front and center at the memorial Adolph Zukor had thrown together in Hollywood a few days before. The event had the dual purpose of memorializing those in the movie industry who had died in filming accidents, under mysterious circumstances and of "accidental" self-inflicted gunshot wounds, and of demonstrating to the world that there was dignity to be found among moving picture folk. The memorial had already been in the works, but when news of Olive Thomas' death reached Hollywood a moving tribute was seamlessly added. The setting was Brunton Studios and Zukor called on William Desmond Taylor, one of the industry's most respected, and seemingly respectable, members to deliver what amounted to a eulogy for its fallen members. The stakes were high; this event would be reported in newspapers around the world and the crusaders for moral decency and church ladies were poised. There were prayers delivered by The Reverend Neal Dodd of Saint Mary of the Angels Episcopal Church, which was attended by many in the motion picture community, and hymns sung by a choir. When Taylor finally spoke to the audience of eight hundred or so, he never mentioned the scandals. In his cultured British accent, Taylor talked about the respect, honor, duty, friendship, and love that was shared within the motion picture community not just by those who had died, but by those who remained. And he accomplished his goal of imbuing the tragedies that had befallen Olive Thomas and the others with dignity as opposed to prurience. Outwardly, Taylor was the poster child for all that Hollywood wanted to project about its citizens. That he had dark secrets of his own was his business. At that point in September 1920, Taylor couldn't have known that his murder, which would take place on the evening of February 1, 1922, would be the third major scandal to rock Hollywood.

Between Olive Thomas' death and William Desmond Taylor's murder was a scandal that would not only shake the Hollywood community to its core, but also deliver devastating ammunition to those who would sit in judgment of its product: the trials of Roscoe "Fatty" Arbuckle.

Exactly a year after Olive Thomas' death, over the Labor Day weekend in September 1921, Arbuckle, one of Hollywood's most popular and successful comedic actors, had taken a break from his hectic career and gone to San Francisco with two friends, actor-director Lowell Sherman and cameraman Fred Fischbach, to cut loose, checking into three suites at the St. Francis Hotel. The trio invited a number of women to join them, including model and bit-part actress Virginia Rappe, whom Arbuckle knew from Hollywood. She was, by all accounts, someone who loved to party with abandon. During the weekend she became seriously ill. There would be speculation that she perhaps became sick from a recent abortion, or possibly from imbibing the questionable Prohibition era alcohol. Regardless, two days after the September 5 party, Maude Delmont, who had met and befriended Virginia at the party, took her to a hospital, where she died a few days later, on September 9, 1921, of peritonitis that developed from a ruptured bladder. After Virginia's death, Delmont claimed that Arbuckle had raped Rappe in spite of the fact that she was not actually present when the alleged sexual assault took place. In fact, because of her extensive criminal background, which included accusations of blackmail and extortion, Maude Delmont never took the stand to testify against Arbuckle in any of his three trials. But that did not stop the San Francisco district attorney Matthew Brady, who had ambitions for the California governorship, from pursuing the case.

The God squad went wild. The events leading up to Roscoe Arbuckle's arrest and subsequent trials fed into every preconceived notion the church ladies and their fellow travelers held, and more. There was sex, booze, drugs, and more sex. And the wages of all this sin? Well, death, of course. First for Virginia Rappe, and then, the moralists fervently hoped, for Arbuckle. In fact, there were calls for his execution from the day the news broke in the press. Those who lined up against Arbuckle were bitterly disappointed that the charge filed was for manslaughter, which took death by hanging off the table. So inflamed was the public that during the first trial someone took a shot at Arbuckle's estranged wife Minta Durfee, who attended the proceedings in support of her husband. After two weeks of testimony of sixty witnesses, eighteen of whom were physicians, the case went to the jury. Five days later the jury declared itself hopelessly deadlocked with a vote of ten-to-two to acquit. A mistrial was declared and the charges were refiled. The drama would continue and would be covered in exhaustive, sensationalized detail by the press, especially William Randolph Hearst's newspapers, which included the *Los Angeles Examiner*. This criminal proceeding was not going to fade from the public eye. The coverage would be there for the duration and would exacerbate the tragedy to such a degree that Arbuckle's innocence alone would never be enough to diffuse the scandal. Which made Hearst happy—he is reported to have said that Arbuckle's trial had sold more newspapers "than any event since the sinking of the *Lusitania*."

In January 1922, a second trial for manslaughter began in San Francisco with the same legal cast and a new jury. If anything, the testimony this time was more sordid than the first. One witness claimed that San Francisco D.A. Brady had forced her to lie; another, a studio security guard who claimed that Arbuckle had bribed him to get a key to Rappe's dressing room, was revealed under cross-examination by the defense to have an open charge against him for sexually assaulting an eight-year-old girl. Once again the jury deadlocked ten-to-two for acquittal. And, once again, San Francisco D.A. Brady refiled the charges.

For the third trial Arbuckle's defense team went on the offensive. Rappe's scandalous past and tragic medical history of serial abortions was introduced. Arbuckle's defense attorney made a point of the fact that Maude Delmont, the woman who had initiated the criminal case, had never been called as a witness. The case went to the jury on April 12, 1922; six minutes later, they returned a unanimous verdict of not guilty that included an apology that read: "Acquittal is not enough for Roscoe Arbuckle. We feel that a great injustice has been done him . . . for there was not the slightest proof adduced to connect him in any way with the commission of crime." That wasn't exactly true. After three trials for manslaughter, Arbuckle pled guilty to one count of violating the Volstead Act. He paid a $500 fine. But he was free, exonerated of all charges of harming Virginia Rappe. He was also broke. Arbuckle owed more than $700,000 (almost $10 million in 2017 dollars) to his legal team. And in spite of his innocence, his career was finished.

Innocent or not, the damage was done. Arbuckle's exoneration meant less than nothing to those who occupied the high ground of righteous rectitude. The trials, with the relentless, speculative press coverage, had given them a moral platform so elevated, nothing short of Arbuckle's ruin would sate them. Theater owners who attempted to show Arbuckle films faced boycotts and worse. Adolph Zukor's studio, which had a number of unreleased Arbuckle films ready to go, was faced with the prospect that it would not be able to recoup its investment. In the end, Hollywood, or more specifically Adolph Zukor, served up Roscoe Arbuckle as a sacrificial lamb to appease the moral high grounders. It was that or face the reality that the religious zealots might use Arbuckle's fall as the excuse to seize full control in perpetuity over movie content.

As the trials progressed, Hollywood producers, especially Zukor, had been fighting a multifront war against those calling for censorship of movie content. The producers would have to concede defeat in the battle to reclaim Arbuckle's career if they were to win a truce against interference from those who wished to exert censorship control. And it fell to Will H. Hays, recently of the Harding administration and newly anointed head of the Motion Picture Producers and Distributors of America censor board, to bring down the hammer on Roscoe Arbuckle. It's to Hays' credit, and the self-appointed morals enforcers' eternal shame, that he banned Arbuckle's films, past, present, and future, from American screens with great reluctance, and in the aftermath did his best to get Arbuckle reinstated. Hays was himself a deeply religious man and what he had to do to appease the self-righteous howls from the hinterlands never sat well with him, because Arbuckle had been found not guilty. It wasn't fair and it wasn't right, but that didn't mean it wasn't necessary to keep the wheels of Hollywood turning with minimal interference from censors of all stripes.[7]

Arbuckle's prominent Hollywood friends did their best to offer support. From London, Charlie Chaplin, who had kept his Leftist leanings and pacifism under wraps during World War One, told the press that he couldn't, and wouldn't, believe that Arbuckle had anything to do with Virginia Rappe's death. Buster Keaton delivered a public statement supporting Arbuckle's innocence, for which he received a tepid rebuke from his studio. Arbuckle's estranged wife, and frequent co-star, Minta Durfee attended the trial and was steadfast in her belief that Roscoe was innocent. After their divorce, Durfee continued to call her ex-husband one of the nicest men in the world. Even Will Hays wrote Arbuckle a letter of apology, something that the fallen actor treasured.[8] But in spite of these measures, as well as his work under the pseudonym William Goodrich, Arbuckle never regained the prominence, or the bank balance, he had once enjoyed.

What happened to Arbuckle was a rude awakening to his fellow stars. For Roscoe Arbuckle, even though he was innocent—and wealthy—the scandal inflamed by the press was taken as proof of the perfidy of Hollywood and everyone who toiled there. In spite of the public's continued enthusiasm for his comedic movies, his career was effectively ended.

Just before Roscoe Arbuckle's sojourn through the criminal court came to an end, the third major Hollywood scandal of the early 1920s hit the filmmaking community with the January 1922 murder of actor-turned-director William Desmond Taylor, the same English-accented paragon of cultured reticence who had eulogized Olive Thomas in September 1920. And unlike Olive Thomas and Roscoe Arbuckle, this scandal was geographically at Mary Pickford's doorstep.

Once again the press went wild with speculation. The studios were forced to manage yet another messy scandal that could feed into the moralists' frenzy against the movie industry. In fact, representatives from Taylor's studio showed up to remove many of Taylor's personal belongings at about the same time the police arrived, which meant the studio became privy to Taylor, and his friends', secrets. The investigation ran into roadblocks at almost every turn. Likely suspects in the Hollywood community turned to their friend District Attorney Thomas Lee Woolwine, who otherwise was known as a reform-minded prosecutor who targeted public corruption, to protect them from being interviewed by the police. (Woolwine's brother lived in Beverly Hills.) Detectives in the Los Angeles Police Department turned to cooperative members of the press to plant stories with the hope of flushing out the individuals they felt were being protected by the district attorney. The police also secured the services of private investigators to circumvent laws.

Taylor, who was a very private individual, had secrets. Secrets that, had he lived, quite probably would have been known by very few. Taylor had changed his name before coming to Hollywood. He lived in Hollywood as a bachelor, but he had been married and had a daughter. He was homosexual, carrying on a long-term relationship with set designer George James Hopkins, who would go on to win multiple Academy Awards for *A Streetcar Named Desire, My Fair Lady, Who's Afraid of Virginia Woolf?,* and *Hello, Dolly!* Taylor was a kind man, loyal to his friends, and he spent most evenings reading. Mabel Normand, who co-starred with Roscoe Arbuckle in many films, was a close friend and confidante—although not a lover—and credits Taylor with helping her overcome her dependence on cocaine.[9] Taylor was universally liked and admired in Hollywood, as rare an occurrence in the 1920s as it is today. And yet, after his death, his life was put under a microscope, his secrets revealed, and his legacy eviscerated. All because he had the very bad luck to be shot dead in his home late one night by a killer who, considering there was no evidence of forced entry or theft, must have been known to Taylor, but was never identified and apprehended. At first the police suspected Henry Peavey, his valet, a flamboyant gay man of color, who discovered Taylor's body but who had a rock-solid alibi for the night before when his boss was killed. Then the police focused on Charlotte Shelby, the mother of Mary Miles Minter, a young actress who had deluded herself into thinking Taylor was in love with her. The suspicion of Shelby was reinforced by D.A. Woolwine's obvious interference in protecting Mary and her mother, Charlotte (who had chosen her last name to infer that they were direct descendants of Kentucky's first governor, Isaac Shelby).[10] Members of the LAPD investigating Taylor's murder who wanted to question Mary Miles Minter and Charlotte Shelby and were prevented from doing so, drew the conclusion that there must be a reason Woolwine was protecting them and that reason was they were either guilty or complicit. Mary Miles Minter and Charlotte Shelby were frequently mentioned in the press in association with the case, which must have driven Mary Pickford, whose mother's name was also Charlotte, to distraction at the thought readers might think she was somehow involved. Because the studio had disturbed the crime scene by removing many of Taylor's possessions, and other investigators were tripping over themselves trying to either set up those they thought were guilty or obfuscate suspicion from those they wanted to protect, the person who actually shot Taylor slipped under the investigative radar and was never discovered. William J. Mann, who wrote the engrossing *Tinseltown: Murder, Morphine, and Madness at the Dawn of Hollywood* about the Taylor murder, posited that the actual murderer was a man known as Blackie Madsen, one half of a blackmail duo that was in cahoots with a down-and-out actress named Margaret "Gibby" Gibson, who had targeted Taylor. According to Mann, the murder was a shakedown gone wrong.[11]

Fame was the catalyst for the over-the-top attention. People of all walks of life behaved badly, often reprehensively and sometimes criminally. For the socially secure, a big bank account and connections often mitigated repercussions for bad behavior. When ordinary people got into trouble with the law, got into debt, or associated with, and often married, the wrong people, their misfortune went unexamined by strangers. Olive Thomas liked to party and in all likelihood she ingested mercury bichloride accidently, but she would forever be associated with the salacious details of her demise. (Not to mention the world was now aware that Jack Pickford had syphilis.) Being innocent hadn't saved Roscoe Arbuckle—scandal had robbed him of his career. It wasn't enough that someone murdered William Desmond Taylor—the aftermath deprived him of his dignity as well as his legacy. Everyone has secrets they would prefer remain hidden, and that included Mary Pickford and Douglas Fairbanks. And the greater a person's fame, the more vulnerable that person was to the revelation of their secrets. It's very possible that Pickford had an abortion while married to Owen Moore; she certainly had carried on a long, extramarital affair with Fairbanks, who was at the time a married man. Fairbanks may have been the last, but he probably wasn't Pickford's only lover while she was married to Moore, and Pickford hadn't been Douglas Fairbanks' only dalliance while he was married to his first wife, Beth Sully, either. Douglas Fairbanks' father was Jewish, a fact that haunted him, and to be fair, the rampant anti-Semitism of the time reinforced his desire to keep his religious background just that, in the background. Pickford must have realized that if she became either the victim or, unlikely as it may seem, the perpetrator of a crime, nothing would protect her privacy entirely. But she also must have felt that living in a city separate from Los Angeles, as well as the geographic distance from Hollywood that Beverly Hills offered her and her friends, could act as a shield from the excesses of both the press and the Los Angeles Police Department.

Mary Pickford and Douglas Fairbanks could have lived in a beautiful home anywhere in the greater Los Angeles area. It was no accident that they remained cocooned in Beverly Hills, a city that would offer them a buffer from the meaner surrounding municipality and its bureaucracy.

7

Meanwhile, in Beverly Hills . . .

⸻◇◇◇⸻

B y the early 1920s Beverly Hills was running out of readily available water. The principals of the Rodeo Land and Water Company learned that they had to be careful what they wished for. Their bottom line depended on land sales picking up and the building of fine homes to commence, which would, in turn, attract more residents. But the sources of water that had sustained the city when the population was negligible—and for which Rodeo's utility company was responsible for providing—were beginning to feel the strain. And the emerging glitterati of the motion picture industry who were following Doug and Mary to live in Beverly Hills weren't helping, what with their grand homes that included not just lush gardens and fully grown trees, but *waterfalls* as well.

As part of the enticement to make its land development in a region that was notoriously water parched attractive to potential buyers, the Rodeo Land and Water Company had promised to provide water and municipal services to the city's residents for fifteen years. That promise of readily available local water for robust, sustained growth over the next decade and a half was one that it probably knew couldn't be kept even as it made it. The truth was, the Rodeo Land and Water Company had found it was easy to get into the water business when it wanted to sell land, but hard to get out of it when the demand for water exceeded the readily available supply. After all, Rodeo was first and foremost in the business of land development.

Since the Rodeo Land and Water Company no longer wanted to be in the water and sewage business, but was unwilling to turn over the utilities to the Beverly Hills city government without being compensated, the remedy seemed obvious: Beverly Hills should join the City of Los Angeles and be entitled to share the abundant water that was flowing into the city from the Owens Valley. For the Rodeo Land and Water Company, proposing an election to annex to Los Angeles was all about the water, something that had been a motivating factor in the city's politics since before Beverly Hills incorporated. It had been all about the water in 1900, when, after failing to find enough oil to make drilling economically feasible but finding ample amounts of groundwater, the Amalgamated Oil Company reinvented itself as the Rodeo Land and Water Company, with the idea of developing what had originally been Maria Valdez's Mexican land grant and then the Hammel and Denker Ranch into a residential community.

Writing a series of articles on the history of Beverly Hills for the *Beverly Hills Citizen*, B. J. Firminger, who had been the Beverly Hills city clerk at the time, opined that the prospect of annexation to Los Angeles and the subsequent vote could have been avoided if cooler heads in the city's government had prevailed. When the water crisis began in earnest in the early 1920s, the Rodeo Land and Water Company suggested selling its Beverly Hills Utility Company along with the water rights and distribution systems to the City of Beverly Hills at a price set by the State of California's Railroad Commission, which at the time was the government agency in charge of public utility price negotiations. But according to Firminger, there was a group of "hot heads who felt the Rodeo people were under an obligation to furnish water without the penalty of annexation to the City of Los Angeles; that if [the Rodeo Land and Water Company] was unable to or unwilling to do this it should turn over [the Beverly Hills Utility Company] to the city without cost."[1]

Upon hearing the demand that it turn over the Beverly Hills Utility Company to the city without receiving payment, the Rodeo Land and Water Company exercised the nuclear option: It proposed annexation to Los Angeles and the elimination of Beverly Hills as an independent city entirely. During the tense period that followed, legal lines were drawn at meetings of the Beverly Hills trustees, as the city council was called. Paul E. Schwab, who would succeed Silsby Spalding as mayor of Beverly Hills, asked the trustees of the city to file suit against Rodeo Land and Water's utility arm to compel it to find the water it was legally obligated to provide by either drilling new wells or purchasing from other water companies. Upon learning of the potential lawsuit, the Rodeo Land and Water Company hired Francis Haney, considered one of the state's top criminal attorneys, because it thought it might lose the court case.[2]

The message from representatives of the Rodeo Land and Water Company's Beverly Hills Utility Company to the citizens of the city they served was dire: The city was running out of fresh spring water; joining up with Los Angeles was the only way out and they had the reports to prove it. The water coming from the newer wells in the southern part of the city contained sulfur, with its attending odor of rotten eggs. To further build the case for annexation, the quality of this water was being called into question by proxies of the Rodeo Land and Water Company. In late 1922 the California State Board of Health in Sacramento was asked to hold hearings on the quality of the water from the new sources.[3] Faced with the question of what could be done about the odious water from the new wells, the Rodeo Land and Water Company had a ready answer: annex to Los Angeles and share in the bounty of its fresh Owens Valley water. And even though the Rodeo Land and Water Company eventually found out from local hydraulic engineers that more water could be obtained—for a price—it didn't feel the need to share this fact with the City of Beverly Hills in the months leading up to the proposed annexation to Los Angeles.

From the perspective of the Rodeo Land and Water Company, joining the City of Los Angeles seemed like the most reasonable course of action, and its public position was that it couldn't understand why everyone didn't see the situation as it did. Beverly Hills was running out of water and Los Angeles was swimming in the stuff. But Silsby Spalding and the majority of the trustees of the City of Beverly Hills felt otherwise. For one thing, they were acutely aware that the self-interests of the Rodeo Land and Water Company and the City of Beverly Hills were not aligned. And there was not a great deal of trust built up between Beverly Hills and Los Angeles; contentious interactions between them—a fight over improving schools, and Los Angeles running roughshod over the smaller municipality when it ran a pipeline for its water through their city—made a precipitous annexation to Los Angeles seem shortsighted to Beverly Hills' civic leadership.

The dispute over expanding the school had occurred before Beverly Hills incorporated as a city. However, Spalding and his fellow trustees hadn't forgotten the city government's first legal interaction with Los Angeles, which in turn was also its first internal conflict with the Rodeo Land and Water Company. On April 25, 1914, about three months after the city's incorporation papers had been signed in Sacramento, Los Angeles, with a right-of-way purchased from the Rodeo Land and Water Company before the city's incorporation, began laying a water pipe across Coldwater Canyon within the boundaries of Beverly Hills without obtaining permission from the city to do so. In an illuminating discussion of the early history of Beverly Hills that took place in April 1946 among some of the city's early movers and shakers—including Ivan Traucht; Raymond Page; Arthur Pillsbury, who had been Beverly Hills' first city engineer; Stanley Anderson of the Beverly Hills Hotel; and Claude Kimball—the men discussed some of the shenanigans that took place before the decision to bring the idea of annexation to Los Angeles to a vote.[4] According to Pillsbury, Los Angeles didn't get the pipeline across the city's land without a fight that included Pillsbury and friends approaching the location of the pipeline and taking an armed stance.[5] Cooler heads eventually prevailed and restraining orders and injunctions were filed by Beverly Hills city trustees against Los Angeles. The Rodeo Land and Water Company, which had sold the right-of-way to Los Angeles before the city had incorporated, entered the fray by bringing pressure on the Beverly Hills trustees to cooperate, and the first friction between it and the Beverly Hills city government arose. The Beverly Hills trustees responded, "The government of the City of Beverly Hills has been vested in a board of trustees separate and distinct from your company, over which we do not believe you have any right, legally or morally, or exercise control."[6]

The case went to court and, in spite of what Beverly Hills' attorneys felt was black letter state law, Superior

Court Judge Louis R. Works found in favor of Los Angeles. The larger city, Judge Works reasoned, had the greater need. What wasn't said, but could certainly be inferred, was that the larger city had the greater political muscle. Beverly Hills would have to endure water owned by the City of Los Angeles rushing through its jurisdiction without the benefit of receiving a single drop. The only comfort that Arthur Pillsbury took from doing his best to prevent the pipeline going across the land was the satisfaction of holding up the process and, according to Pillsbury, raising William Mulholland's ire when Pillsbury took the stand in court.[7]

(Arthur Pillsbury and William Mulholland may have clashed in court over the pipeline case in 1914, but the two men had been on good terms previously. When Pillsbury ran into what he thought were potentially catastrophic difficulties building one of Beverly Hills' first reservoirs in Coldwater Canyon, which collected water from the canyon's artesian spring, he consulted with Mulholland. The water was seeping out of the reservoir he was building faster than it was flowing in and Pillsbury thought he was going to have to go back to the Rodeo Land and Water Company to ask for more money to rebuild. Mulholland provided him with a simple solution, suggesting Pillsbury go down to the brickyard in Santa Monica and get some clay, dry it out, and then let the dried clay sink down into the structure and seal the cracks. As of 1946 when Pillsbury was telling the story, the reservoir had held and was still in use.)

Spalding especially—even though he was the second-largest stockholder in the Rodeo Land and Water Company through his wife—was convinced that keeping Beverly Hills a separate city would pay huge dividends in the future by delivering to its citizens more bang for their tax dollars. Not to mention retaining control over the land use and the schools. The city's Board of Trustees had to look no further than Hollywood to see how an independent city could be absorbed into the larger metropolis with little regard for any promises Los Angeles might make. And according to the statute that outlined the procedure for annexation, any city that wished to join Los Angeles went into the marriage without knowing how large of a burden the outstanding bonds it was responsible for would be. At the time of the proposed annexation, Los Angeles had more than $80 million in outstanding bond debt, a sum that translates into $1.5 billion 2017 dollars.

The battle over annexation between the city trustees and the Rodeo Land and Water Company raged on more or less in public, but there was also plenty of subterfuge and secret backroom dealings going on behind the scenes.

Those determined, not to mention prominent, Beverly Hills residents who gathered in 1946 to reminisce about the early days of Beverly Hills were opposed to what the Rodeo Land and Water Company was attempting to do before Mary Pickford and her team of fellow silent screen stars were on board for the fight. The question was, would they have enough influence to prevail without the help of the stars? Considering other cities and unincorporated areas that had agreed to annexation before and after Beverly Hills' 1923 vote—including Hollywood in 1910 and Venice in 1925—the glaring difference in the case of Beverly Hills was the celebrity campaign against joining the larger city. (Although, to be fair, Venice also voted against annexation in its first vote on the matter in 1923. Venice's city trustees continued the drumbeat for annexation with subsequent votes until they got the result they wanted.)

During that April 1946 meeting, Stanley Anderson recalled having recently lunched at the Brown Derby restaurant and run into William Joyce, at whose home the anti-annexationists had gathered in early 1923. While the two were reminiscing, Joyce reminded Anderson that at a dinner Joyce had hosted, the group had raised $52,000 to fight the Rodeo Land and Water Company's bid to join Los Angeles. The anti-annexation group was under considerable pressure,

Joyce reminded Anderson. After hearing about Joyce's anti-annexation gathering, Burton Green had one of the Rodeo Land and Water Company's employees, Harrison Lewis, go to Joyce's house to persuade him to abandon the anti-annexationists and join the pro-annexation camp. Joyce, thinking on his feet, realized he should have a witness to what was going to be said, deflected the visit, and insisted that Lewis come back the following evening. The anti-annexation group needed reinforcements to combat what they had come to feel were underhanded and dubious dealings that the Rodeo Land and Water Company was engaged in. They needed a big gun: The anti-annexation camp needed someone like the universally respected Silsby Spalding, who as a Beverly Hills trustee as well as an heir to the Canfield estate's considerable holdings in Rodeo Land and Water, a position that was second only to Burton Green, gave him a foot in both camps. It was Silsby Spalding whom Joyce invited to listen to the pitch from the pro-annexation camp. While Harrison Lewis was bending William Joyce's ear about the reasons Beverly Hills would be better off joining the larger city, Silsby Spalding was listening and doing a slow burn in the next room. A previous incident during a meeting at the Rodeo School, where Spalding was booed by employees of Rodeo Land and Water Company, had made him mad enough to make a late-night stop at Stanley Anderson's house, wake Anderson up, and declare about the anti-annexation effort, "I am with you in this. I will put money into it." Between his reception at the Rodeo School and whatever it was Spalding heard Lewis, the Rodeo Land and Water Company man, say to William Joyce, Spalding had become stoutly anti-annexation. And it was an opinion Spalding freely shared with his fellow Beverly Hills City trustees. Firminger writes of a trustee meeting open to the public. Spalding asked those in the audience to step outside while the trustees went into executive session. Those who had exited the building couldn't hear what was being said, but they could see through the uncurtained windows that Sil Spalding's fist hit the table and "that he spoke with considerable emphasis."[8]

Leaning on prominent anti-annexation residents wasn't the entirety of the Rodeo Land and Water Company's duplicity, though. At this 1946 meeting, Stanley Anderson described how he discovered that the purported need for annexation to Los Angeles to ensure a ready supply of water was baseless. As someone who was anti-annexation, Anderson had met with J. B. Lippincott, one of the region's best-known hydraulic engineers, to see if there was potentially more water to be pumped in Beverly Hills. According to Anderson's account, when he arrived at the engineer's office, Lippincott was in a meeting, but offered to let Anderson see the file on the project. That's when Anderson discovered evidence that Lippincott's hydraulic engineering services had already been secured by the Rodeo Land and Water Company and a report had been written and delivered to Burton Green. The file was a revelation to Anderson, to say the least. What he found out was that a year before proposing annexation, Burton Green had received a report from Lippincott indicating that "they could develop enough water for 30,000 people."[9] Anderson surreptitiously pocketed a copy of Lippincott's letter to Burton Green, proof that Green knew well and good, and had known for as long as a year, that more water could be obtained for Beverly Hills without annexation to Los Angeles. Anderson showed the letter to Spalding as proof that while it may have been in the best interests of Rodeo Land and Water Company for Beverly Hills to annex itself to Los Angeles, it wasn't necessarily in the best interest of the city. Rodeo Land and Water wasn't telling the city the whole story.

In the autumn of 1922, while the plans for transferring the city's water utility company were before the State Railroad Commission in Sacramento, because the Rodeo Land and Water Company had refused to transfer the utility company it had set up to provide services to the City of Beverly Hills without compensation, the question of where Beverly Hills would acquire additional water was heating up back home. At a meeting held by the Beverly Hills Civic Club, attorney Force Parker, who had been hired by the trustees of the City of Beverly Hills, read a report outlining three solutions to the impending water crisis. Parker's report favored the acquisition of twelve wells from the Hollywood Union Water Company for a cost of about $350,000. According to the report, the wells would provide enough water to supply a city of 250,000. For a bond measure of $500,000, Parker stated, "Beverly Hills could own its own water supply, have fire protection and enough water left over to sell, if desired."[10] The other two solutions included compelling the Rodeo Land and Water Company to expand its wells and reduce its rates, or annexation to Los Angeles. The attendees of this particular meeting were firmly in the camp of keeping Beverly Hills independent, but stopped short of formally adopting the idea that the city should obtain its own municipal water system. Action was postponed until after the State Railroad Commission ruled on the case of the transfer of the Rodeo Land and Water Company's utility company to the City of Beverly Hills that was currently before it.[11]

To be fair to the Rodeo Land and Water Company and its water utility, though, it's also safe to say that they had no idea just how over the top the homes in the city's near future were going to be. But with William Mulholland's monumental aqueduct project recently completed at the time Beverly Hills incorporated (it was completed and water began to flow in November 1913), it's quite possible that the principals of the Rodeo Land and Water Company thought they saw a way out of the almost certain water shortage whether it came sooner or later. All through 1913, some of the region's smaller cities were holding out hope that the water flowing down to Los Angeles would be available to them. Other municipalities, from Long Beach and Santa Monica to the south and west, and Pasadena and Glendora to the north and east, had expressed interest in buying the "extra" water, as if there could be such a thing,[12] and having Los Angeles figure out a way to deliver it. Mulholland wasn't necessarily opposed to selling water, but he didn't think that building water supply infrastructure for other municipalities was the responsibility of the City of Los Angeles. In Mulholland's opinion, "If a community wanted to be part of the [City of Los Angeles] water system, the solution was simple . . . become part of the city, pay city taxes and enjoy city services."[13] However, the cities like Beverly Hills that were looking for water from the Owens Valley weren't keen on being absorbed into Los Angeles for a variety of reasons that included control of their schools and land-use issues. As for getting into the business of negotiating contracts with other cities and selling water, Mulholland, a civil servant who had no personal financial stake in what was, after all, a municipal water department that was owned by the City of Los Angeles, was at best ambivalent. He was "more interested in seeing [Los Angeles] grow than he was in getting into the water sales business."[14]

Not everyone in L.A.'s Department of Water and Power felt the same way. S. C. Graham, the new DWP water commissioner, proposed a project dubbed the "high line" that would be a water delivery system to the San Gabriel Valley to the east, for which Los Angeles would charge a premium on the water to recoup the cost of building the conduit. Not only did the idea of delivering water to the entire region not sit well with Mulholland, it violated the City of Los Angeles Charter. An election was held to amend the charter and it passed by a significant margin. Pasadena and Los Angeles began negotiating for the high line to bring water east. Not so fast, said the Los Angeles city attorneys. They determined that, legally,

Between the late eighteenth and mid-nineteenth centuries, Beverly Hills was Rodeo de las Aguas, one rancho among many.

Maria Valdez lived on Rodeo de las Aguas, which she inherited from her husband in the 1830s. *(The Beverly Hills Historical Society)*

It was easy for the principals of the Rodeo Land and Water Company, four of whom are pictured above (clockwise from top left, Charles Canfield, Henry E. Huntington, Max Whittier, and Burton Green) to get into the water business to sell land. It was harder to find water beyond what they could gather in the Franklin Canyon Reservoir *(top). (The Beverly Hills Historical Society)*

In 1918, the concept of "movie star" was barely a thing, and yet Mary Pickford, pictured at right, along with Douglas Fairbanks, Charlie Chaplin, and Marie Dressler, became the main attraction for Treasury Secretary William McAdoo's Third Liberty Bond tour during World War One. The opening ceremony in Washington, D.C, raised three million dollars alone. *(Cari Beauchamp)*

Mary Pickford handily outsold her fellow Liberty Bond fund-raisers. Pickford would exhort the crowds to buy bonds, even going so far as to auction off one of her famous curls for $15,000 in Chicago. *(Cari Beauchamp)*

Mary Pickford, as "America's Sweetheart," may have been marketed as innocence personified, but she was financially savvy and politically astute.
(Getty Images/Hulton Archive)

The lush-lawn domesticity of Doug and Mary with two of their dogs at home at Pickfair belies the isolation and rusticity of the wilds of Beverly Hills. Neighbors, while few and far between, were also well known to the famous couple. Exactly how they liked it. *(Doug and Mary at Pickfair, courtesy of Cari Beauchamp; aerial shot of Pickfair and its neighbors, courtesy of the collection of Allison Burnett)*

Charlie Blair would eventually become the first police chief of Beverly Hills, but at the time of the 1923 annexation election, he was a fresh-faced patrolman who made his rounds by bicycle. *(The Beverly Hills Historical Society)*

Beverly Hills' impending vote on annexation was not without controversy, and a bit of violence. Two months before the election, an "infernal device" was sent to Al Murphy, the pro-annexation editor of *The Beverly Hills News*. After a few days of torrid press coverage that stretched across the country, the whole incident was reduced to being described as a hoax. *(Detail of the front page of the February 27, 1923, Los Angeles Examiner)*

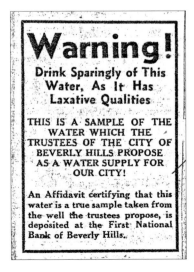

With the exception of the purported bomb sent to *The Beverly Hills News*, the competing campaigns for and against annexation were pretty tame. Mary Pickford and the rest of her anti-annexationists kept their efforts low key with no hijinks. The pro-annexation camp saved their one stunt for the day before the election, when a bottle of sulfurous water was deposited on the doorstep of every Beverly Hills home with a note attached. *(A facsimile of the note courtesy of The Beverly Hills Historical Society)*

Because it's located on a traffic island in the middle of the busy intersection of Olympic Boulevard and South Beverly Drive, most of the residents of Beverly Hills don't realize that this sculpture, entitled "Celluloid," memorializes the eight stars who campaigned against the city's annexation to Los Angeles in 1923. *(Jonathan Brown)*

After she helped save her city from annexation to Los Angeles, Mary Pickford remained engaged in the political life of Beverly Hills. Even though she wasn't running for anything, her appearance at the polls at the Beverly Hills Hotel to vote on a bond measure for the city's municipal services is a photo op. *(The Beverly Hills Collection/Robert S. Anderson)*

Will Rogers became the honorary mayor of Beverly Hills in 1926, and it isn't too far-fetched to imagine that, had he not died in an aviation accident in 1935, the man who made a living with his political commentary would have eventually run for elected office. *(The Beverly Hills Collection/Robert S. Anderson)*

the cities that would be receiving water could not pay for the building of the high line; money would have to come from a bond issue in Los Angeles, which would have to be authorized by a special election. Mulholland took a definite stand against the plan. He was adamant that since it was the City of Los Angeles that had made the huge financial commitment to provide itself with water, the water was for use by the citizens of Los Angeles, not to be the product for a water sale and delivery business, whether it was to the west end of the San Fernando Valley or via the high line to Pasadena. "The city should not pay for either of them," he said.[15] The bond issue failed. There would be no high line to bring water to Pasadena, or any other nearby city for that matter.

Just to the west of Los Angeles, as citizens in Beverly Hills contemplated incorporating into an independent city, Burton Green and the other principals of the Rodeo Land and Water Company must have been closely watching the negotiations for the so-called Graham Proposal—the high line's official name—between Los Angeles and San Gabriel Valley cities such as Pasadena and Glendora. It had to have crossed their minds that, quite possibly, this type of approach—contracting to receive Owens Valley water from Los Angeles—could be an economical answer to the water shortage that was sure to come. The machinations were many and complicated, but this Owens Valley water project the City of Los Angeles had undertaken was still a work in progress in all of its permutations. Bringing water to Pasadena and other San Gabriel Valley cities might be a nonstarter because the bond issue to build the high line was voted down, but things could change. For one thing, Mulholland wouldn't be the chief of the Los Angeles waterworks forever; for another, City of Los Angeles water was already flowing through the City of Beverly Hills. And even though Beverly Hills may have lost the case against Los Angeles in court over the pipeline running through its city limits, laws could be changed and litigation revisited.

While they may have known the limitations of the city's water supply, the Rodeo Land and Water Company and its offshoot, the Beverly Hills Utility Company, must have felt they were in a position to bide their time during the city's earliest days when growth was slow. Just how slow? According to Pierce Benedict's 1934 *History of Beverly Hills,* in the city's early days lima beans were still king and, since the harvesting was done haphazardly, right after threshing the stalks for the crop, Beverly Hills was a prime picnicking destination for Los Angelenos who wanted to pick their own beans and "return home with a year's supply."[16] This existence was bucolic. Between the luxurious

Beverly Hills Hotel and quotidian lima bean fields, in the area just south of the hotel in what is now Will Rogers Park, where Beverly and Canon Drives and Sunset Boulevard converge, weekly baseball games were played. There, the hometown team, the Bean Eaters, whose members included Ed Spence, Pierce Benedict, George McBride, and Rodeo Land and Water Company manager Charles Anderson (no relation to the Andersons of the Beverly Hills Hotel), frequently squared off against the Malted-Hoppers from Maier's Brewery in Los Angeles. Public transportation in that time before automobile ownership was common consisted of a "ramshackle Ford driven by a venerable Jew"[17] that ran between the trolley stop and the Beverly Hills Hotel. Eventually the trolley line (one of Henry Huntington's Dinky lines) would continue west along Sunset Boulevard as far as what would become Whittier Drive on Beverly Hills' western edge, with a stop at the Beverly Hills Hotel. By the mid-1920s, the trolley would be no more. The land that had been under the tracks, however, would become one of the most coveted bridle paths in the world.

Before World War One there was a single building in the business district: a combination grocery store, butcher shop, and post office. During World War One a group of Beverly Hills citizens, a mixture of moving picture talent such as Fred Niblo and Charles Ray and local businessmen such as Jake Dansinger, E. E. Spence, Kirk Johnson, William Hunnewell, and Norman Pabst, formed a company and established a community store. It wasn't until just before Christmas of 1920 that Frank Homer opened the town's first drugstore, the eponymous Homer's, which would quickly attain legendary status because of the soon-to-be-hometown celebs who would shop there.

The water pressure, as it were, started to build after the end of World War One and picked up considerably in 1920, the year Mary Pickford and Doug Fairbanks officially took up residence at Pickfair. Mary and Doug weren't the first wealthy people to set up house in the new city; Harry and Virginia Robinson of J.W. Robinson's Department Store, Silsby Spalding, and King Gillette, the razor magnate, preceded them. And they weren't the first movie people, either; Charles Ray and Corinne Griffith (who would eventually spearhead the effort to erect the memorial sculpture honoring those who fought annexation at the intersection of South Beverly Drive and Olympic Boulevard) were there first. But Mary and Doug were the biggest. While Mary and Doug would always be the queen and king of the community, the influx of motion picture royalty either moving into existing homes or buying land to build in Beverly Hills picked up considerably after 1920. Charlie Chaplin was one of the first, wanting to live near his best friend Doug Fairbanks no doubt. He was followed in rapid succession by Will Rogers; Fred Thomson and his wife Frances Marion, who was a scenarist and one of Mary Pickford's closet friends; Theda Bara; Gloria Swanson, who bought King Gillette's home on Crescent Drive; Harold Lloyd; Rudolph Valentino; Tom Mix; Hobart Bosworth, who moved from Hollywood in order to be able to stable his horses at his home, horses being no longer welcome in Hollywood; Buster Keaton; Marion Davies; Wallace Beery, and studio moguls Louis B. Mayer, Carl Laemmle, and Thomas Ince.[18]

There were insinuations that movie-censor-in-chief Will Hays went as far as suggesting to those stars on the rise who might be caught in any sort of scandalous crosshairs that they make their way west to Beverly Hills. Beverly Hills was far enough from the restaurants, clubs, and speakeasies that were springing up across Hollywood and the rest of Los Angeles, as well as the legions of press who made it their business to trawl such locations looking for juicy tidbits, to make it a perfect neighborhood to which the emerging motion picture glitterati could repair. Once in Beverly Hills, the small, discreet combination police and fire department, which had only recently expanded from the lone deputy, Jack Munson, to include Charlie Blair, would know how to best handle any potential for scandal: quietly. In contrast to the honeycombed-with-corruption Los Angeles Police Department, with its full complement of precincts with rank-and-file policemen, their commanding officers, and specialized departments like Homicide staffed with detectives, in the first three years of the 1920s, Beverly Hills had at most three police officers who rode either bicycles or motorcycles. Crime, according to the 1946 conversation among the Beverly Hills old-timers, included Charlie Chaplin refusing to pay his bill from the Beverly Hills Nursery for landscaping done on his new home. His fiancée at the time, actress Pola Negri, ultimately paid. As for the wild parties where underwear and shoes were thrown on the lush lawns, according to Arthur Pillsbury, Blair, who in 1927 became the city's first police chief, would have a word, asking the hosts to "quiet it down a little bit." Blair would then have a couple of drinks at the soiree and the volume of the festivities would abate. He never arrested anyone and, in fact, had never even drawn his weapon from the holster he wore. Which is probably a good thing, because according to Pillsbury, Charlie Blair couldn't hit a target at close range. This may or may not have been attributable to the fact that taking two or three drinks at every stop he made wasn't just confined to the parties of the movie stars. It should also be noted that most of Beverly Hills' earliest denizens were armed, not so much to protect themselves from crime, but because the city's nonhuman population included mountain lions and coyotes, and the occasional deer would get hit by a car and need to be put out of its misery.[19]

In fact, encouragement to move to Beverly Hills probably didn't need to come from Hays, or any other authority figure, for that matter. Much like the celebs of today, the boys and girls—for the most part they were still impossibly young—who made up the first generation of film stars moved in packs. There was no blueprint for them to follow, no code of conduct. It's important to remember that the first moving picture folk who found fame and fortune didn't go into the flickers with the slightest inkling they'd become wealthy movie stars; their intention was simply to make a living. At the beginning, working in moving pictures had been a leap of faith. Many of those who found early fame, including Mary Pickford, Douglas Fairbanks, and the Gish sisters, Lillian and Dorothy, spent years traveling in theater troupes barely earning enough money to cover their expenses. Over and over we can see in recollections from those who had been in the vanguard of the motion picture industry, including Frances Marion's witty *Off with Their Heads*, that these individuals, most of whom had made it to New York and, not unlike today, wore out the sidewalks between theaters auditioning for parts, took a chance on the new medium. In those early days between 1910 and 1916, none of them ever expected flickers to last, let alone expand and evolve into the widespread entertainment medium that it did. Those who took the leap of faith into flickers became a sister- and brotherhood of characters.

But then as now, they felt most comfortable in each other's company and so they sought each other out. They worked the long hours together, roomed together, and kicked up their heels together. They were citizens of their own world and knew the unique culture and language that outsiders didn't and still don't. This clubbiness is something that would never change for the upper stratum of movie stars. It was an exclusive club and the bona fides necessary for entry were working in the movies. The movie stars knew each other, or were more often than not no more than one degree of separation away from each other, and they knew each other's weaknesses and strengths. Then too, the coverage celebrities permitted was a carefully calibrated commodity; unwanted coverage of peccadilloes was avoided at almost all costs. The information provided was only what they—and the studios— wanted the general public to know. What went on behind this barricade was closely guarded and the few breeches—the devastating coverage of Olive Thomas' death, Roscoe Arbuckle's trial, and the investigation into William Desmond's murder—stood out as stark examples of why the stonewalling had to be maintained. And few stars then or now were as good at secrecy and obfuscation as Mary Pickford. She and her fellow motion picture stars were spinning the press in the 1920s; the A-listers of today are still spinning. Those on the outside—fandom and the rest of the general public—know only what the celebrities want us to know. In the early 1920s, the celebrities in Beverly Hills knew each other for the people they actually were, not as the viewing public thought they knew them, by the characters they portrayed. To the legions of women who swooned whenever Rudolph Valentino appeared on the screen, the young Italian dance instructor-turned-silent-screen star was the epitome of a sex symbol. To his fellow stars of the silver screen and Beverly Hills neighbors who knew and rode horses with him, Rudy was a former student of horticulture in Italy who loved his garden, knew the Latin names of all the plants it contained, and dreamed of buying land and starting a vineyard, perhaps in Napa or Sonoma counties in Northern California, in the not-too-distant future.[20]

In Beverly Hills the stars felt free to be themselves. Firmly entrenched in their collective memory was a time in the not-too-distant past when they weren't wanted in Hollywood. Frances Marion, who came to Los Angeles from her hometown of San Francisco to be a poster illustrator for Los Angeles theater impresario Oliver Morosco, describes her initial impressions of 1914 Los Angeles and Hollywood this way:

"After you left the squat dingy railroad station there was little of interest to be seen beyond the old Spanish Mission on the Plaza and a few adobe houses marked by oleander trees and overshadowed by giraffe-like palms. Obviously the city had sprung up helter-skelter without any pattern, for there was more evidence of haste than taste. . . .

"Before reporting to Mr. Morosco, I decided to find an apartment which I could convert into a studio of sorts. There were vacancies galore but tacked over many of the rental signs was this ominous edict: 'No Jews, actors or dogs allowed.' My blood boiled! I had come from a cosmopolitan city where Jews were revered for their contribution to the arts, science and industry. Where actors were welcome as holidays. . . .

"I learned from Mr. Morosco that the barring of actors from the apartment houses referred only to performers in the movies. [According to Mr. Morosco] '. . . [t]housands are trekking west and this is resented by large groups of people, mostly churchgoers, who are forming committees to keep these ragtag and bobtails off the streets and out of our parks.' "[21]

Marion was dumbfounded by this attitude and wondered how "anyone could resent the lively fun [moving picture folk] had brought into this dull environment."[22]

When they became successful, many of the same moving picture ragtag and bobtails remembered their reception in Hollywood, including Marion, who in her writings described herself "instinctively" as identifying with the "underdog" (by which she meant the disparaged members of the young motion picture industry). Marion would go on to join the ranks of the said underdogs two years after she arrived in Los Angeles when she signed a contract with Bosworth, one of Hollywood's first studios and the eventual partner of Marion's first Southern California boss, Oliver Morosco. Those selfsame ragtag and bobtails knew where they weren't wanted and they knew who hadn't wanted them. When they had coin in pocket, Beverly Hills beckoned.

It was never the intention of the men who developed Beverly Hills to create a modest community of small tract homes tucked onto tidy little lots. The idea was always for a luxury development. But in a few very significant ways, the silent screen stars moving to Beverly Hills were a mixed blessing to the developers.

Yes, a few of the neighbors groused about "picture folk," but it wasn't what the newcomers did for a living that would become fateful for Beverly Hills' looming water crisis. They built outsized, luxurious manses designed by the top architects of the time on sprawling acreage that they planted with lush gardens and water-hungry full-grown trees. They installed inground swimming pools. And in a region where water was a precious resource, some even built waterfalls. It's not *that* the stars chose to build in Beverly Hills, it's *how* they built in Beverly Hills that probably accelerated the city's shortage of water resources.

Frances Marion's story of how her home grew from a seven-room California Rancho era–inspired hacienda to a more than twenty-acre spread with multiple structures is a window into this domestic escalation. While they were living in rural New York State, Marion's husband Fred Thomson bought a dapple gray horse with the idea of turning him into an equine movie star. Instead, Joseph P. Kennedy, during his time as a Hollywood producer at FBO pictures, convinced Fred he should star along with the horse. Of course, one horse could not do all the tricks; other dapple grays with individual skill sets (jumping, kneeling, galloping, sidestepping) would have to be procured. Fred hired Wallace Neff, at the time one of the region's top architects, to design and build both the stable for the horses and a bunkhouse for the ranch hands who would see to the horses, both larger than Marion and Thomson's prospective home. Full-grown shade trees were to be hauled to the property and planted. In her memoir, Marion writes of going to check on the project's progress and seeing that a deep, wide ditch was being cut from the top of the hill closest to the riding ring. She asked if it was a firebreak. It wasn't. The excavation was for a waterfall, the resulting spray of which would keep the horses cool. Soon Marion decided that her small adobe hacienda was going to look like a wart next to the grander buildings devoted to the horses and the men who tended to them. To remedy the situation, Frances Marion herself called Wallace Neff to design a bigger house. By the time all was said and done, Frances Marion and Fred Thomson had "built the largest house on the highest hill in Beverly Hills."[23]

Marion and Thomson weren't alone in their over-the-top efforts. According to Marion's memoir, many of the silent screen stars who moved to Beverly Hills built "Temples of Mammon" for themselves. These houses represented a mash-up of architectural styles, often within the same structure, and were furnished as if "Europe disgorged its treasure into our laps: paintings from Paris, antique furniture from Italy and Spain, rugs from Arabia . . . and silver bearing the crests of distinguished English families impoverished by the war."[24] The silent screen nouveaux riches, formerly denizens of homes with stoops and porches, now had lives that revolved around poolside terraces. The arrivistes dug out the native plantings and installed lawns, planted full-grown trees, and added water elements that included fountains, creeks, and artificial waterfalls that brought to mind such water-blessed locations as the English countryside. They had butlers and maids and cooks. In every way possible, they had arrived and Beverly Hills had set the stage.

And so it went. According to Marion, "Houses began to spring up on all the hills like gilded monuments. Every parvenu tried to outdo every other parvenu."[25] All those gilded monuments sucked up water as if there was an unlimited supply of the stuff. There wasn't. And when it was clear that demand was going to exceed supply, instead of paying to get more water, it was the goal of the utility company that was wholly owned by the Rodeo Land and Water Company, not the city, to hand Beverly Hills to the tender mercies of Los Angeles.

8

"California's Floating Kidney Transplanted from the Midwest"

———◆◆◆———

Writing in her journal the day before she left San Francisco, Frances Marion described Los Angeles—the city with which Beverly Hills was contemplating annexing itself—as "California's Floating Kidney Transplanted from the Midwest."[1]

But Los Angeles' image depended heavily on who was viewing it and from where. Bolstered by chamber-of-commerce advertising touting the healthy environment and the boxcars arriving on the East Coast full of golden oranges that acted as globe-like ambassadors of the sweet life, many saw Los Angeles (mostly in their mind's eye from a perch thousands of miles away) as a temperate paradise with ripe fruit falling from the trees directly into outstretched palms. As you got closer, though, the view changed considerably. To wit: San Francisco's already tetchy opinion of the city down south, and certain residents of Beverly Hills, the small city that sat to the west of downtown, who contemplated joining Los Angeles' sprawling mass with horror. Even in the Jazz Age–Roaring Twenties fever dream of bootleg booze and overnight stardom on the silver screen, when it seemed that life would always be as perfect as the weather, doubt about the fulfillment of the promise of the so-called California Dream, like a drop of ink hitting water, was beginning to spread. The scandals of the previous three years that involved celebrity, drugs, sex, and death were harbingers that Los Angeles was well on its way to cultivating a unique, often porous, juxtaposition of high- and low-life that seemed to present itself unabashedly in stark relief in the bright sunshine, but could only really be understood in the corresponding shadows. Los Angeles wasn't a city on the cusp anymore; sometime during the early 1920s it had slipped over into a manic depression from which many say it still suffers. It was the conflicted, contradictory atmosphere that by the beginning of the next few decades would beguile writers from all over the world and lure them to the noir side of paradise. For reasons that ranged from aversion to the press to maintaining control over city services—which included a small, compliant police force—those Beverly Hills residents who opposed joining Los Angeles wanted to keep their Elysium intact and separate. Maybe it was reluctance to accept change, or perhaps without being consciously aware of it, they were reading the tea leaves that told the future of the large city that surrounded them, which was determined to be a teeming metropolis.

In the first quarter of the twentieth century, Los Angeles was both very different and depressingly the same as the rest of the country's big cities. It was different in that while other cities with large populations had evolved over centuries, Los Angeles had exploded almost entirely within the decade between 1910 and 1920. New York, the biggest city in the United States, had grown in fits and starts from a seventeenth-century Dutch trading post at the southern tip of the island of Manhattan; as recently as the middle of the nineteenth century, Harlem in the north part of Manhattan had still been farmland. San Francisco had begun as North America's deepwater port on the Pacific, and had grown in spurts, first after the discovery of gold in 1848 and then after the arrival of Chinese laborers for the transcontinental railroad at the end of the Civil War in 1865; its population would decline after the 1906 earthquake.

Before the transcontinental railroad was completed in 1869, travel to California from points east was a grueling ordeal. The choices were overland by wagon train or stagecoach, or an ocean voyage of months that involved circumnavigating South America; the Panama Canal would not be completed until 1914. Once the railroad to California was complete, to get to Los Angeles travelers needed to take another train south from the railroad's western terminus of Alameda across the bay from San Francisco. There wasn't a direct rail line from east of the Mississippi to Los Angeles until the Southern Pacific began service in the early 1880s. When the first train travelers arrived, it was to a much smaller city that gave little hint of the growth to come. At the turn of the twentieth century, Los Angeles struggled to find enough potable water for its 100,000 citizens. By 1910, the population had tripled to 319,000, and it almost doubled again to 576,000 by 1920. The growth wasn't pretty. Even in its earliest days, there was a temporariness about the city. Things just weren't built to last in Los Angeles. It could have been because of the climate—mild winters didn't require substantial construction to keep the elements at bay—but perhaps it was because Los Angeles always seemed transitory. Even though hundreds of thousands of people ended up settling in Los Angeles, the city always gave the impression it was more of a way station than a destination. Urban planning, beyond the most rudimentary zoning for business, industry, and residential, was more of an afterthought than an initial approach and often ignored. Like London, Los Angeles was cobbled together from villages connected by a remarkably robust public transport system, only in the case of the City of the Queen of the Angels, there was an appalling lack of charm and aesthetic appeal. Frances Marion's initial impression was that the city had sprung up helter-skelter "with more haste than taste."[2] Other cities in the region that had enjoyed a more tempered growth—Pasadena, for example—were lovely, replete with tree-lined residential streets of California Craftsman bungalows, interspersed by parks. Los Angeles' architectural gems, of which there were—and still are—quite a few, became lost in the chaos of a boomtown mentality that saw neighborhoods spring up almost overnight. Because they were often hastily built with shoddy materials and poor craftsmanship, even homes in "better" neighborhoods quickly turned shabby. Just as quickly, however, new housing sprang up. The city's growing population, especially its wealthier segment, never lacked for bright, shiny new digs.

Los Angeles not only lacked aesthetic appeal in its architecture and planning, it was dirty and smelly. By 1920, the city and its adjacent communities produced almost 25 percent of the world's petroleum. Oil production is a filthy business, from its exploration and extraction to its refinement and transport.

In some ways it's understandable why the Rodeo Land and Water Company didn't see a problem annexing Beverly Hills to Los Angeles. After all, the company had originally been called Amalgamated Oil and its intention had been to find and extract petroleum from the land it purchased. Becoming land developers had been plan B when the oil under the ground failed to materialize.

Los Angeles had evolved differently in its growth, but it was depressingly similar to other large American cities when it came to political corruption and organized crime—similar, but not quite the same. Like every other city in the United States, Prohibition boosted the scope and reach of organized crime in Los Angeles and encouraged its companion, political corruption, to move from the fringes to center stage, corroding the integrity of every level of the criminal justice system along the way. Unlike its counterparts to the east, though, organized crime in Los Angeles wasn't in the hands of mobs based on ethnic origins that had evolved along with the cities where they lived, like the Irish, Italians, and Jews in New York City, Boston, and Chicago. Los Angeles in the 1920s did organized crime its own way. It had its own syndicate,

The System, that in its low-profile way controlled boot-legging, prostitution, gambling, and loan-sharking, but instead of gangs that maintained monetary rela-tionships with politicians, L.A.'s crime and political corruption were one and the same. As of 1920, crime and graft were centralized in Los Angeles' City Hall and the LAPD was an active partner. It was a civi-lized arrangement made up of prominent men who made sure businesses on both sides of the law were working smoothly. The era of Mickey Cohen was still more than ten years in the future. In the early 1920s, there were no shootouts in the streets pitting law en-forcement against machine-gun-toting hoodlums. City government, the business community, and police all participated in the graft and glad-handing that made their world go round, and they did it without draw-ing undue attention to themselves. Political fixer Kent Kane Parrot, who had played football at USC and whose first wife was the screenwriter Mary O'Hara, had set the stage for The System through his unique, though nefarious, coalition building that brought together such disparate delegations as church lead-ers, liberals, conservatives, teetotalers, and bootleg-gers.[3] In 1921 Parrot engineered the election of George Cryer, someone who was sympathetic to an enlightened approach toward vice, as mayor of L.A. In Charlie Crawford, who earlier in the twentieth century had created a fully integrated approach to crime in Seattle before moving to Los Angeles in 1910 to open The Maple Bar, which became a front for the criminal enterprise he subsequently built, Parrot discovered a man who understood the always subtly shifting ground that was the territory where political influence met criminal activities. Crawford was the type of guy Parrot needed to perfect The System. Between the two of them, money from all manner of illegal activities, from prostitution and loan-sharking to bootlegging and protection, would flow from Crawford to Parrot to be disseminated through City Hall and the LAPD headquarters.

The few reformers who made it from the ballot to office, including Thomas Lee Woolwine, who was the Los Angeles County district attorney at the time of the annexation attempt, didn't enjoy long tenures in office. Even Woolwine, while overall an honest prosecutor and a pillar of virtue when compared with his fellow elected officials, was not above protecting his friends from being investigated in the murder of William Desmond Taylor. Woolwine remains a paragon of integrity, though, when contrasted with his successor, Asa Keyes, who was convicted of bribery in the Julian Pete (short for Julian Petroleum) scandal, which was a homegrown Los Angeles pyramid scheme in which citizens from all walks of life were fleeced out of millions of dollars.

For the most part, the residents of Beverly Hills were neither innocents nor fools; they were wealthy, worldly, and under no illusions. What went on in Los Angeles' City Hall, in the police precincts, and the courts was no secret. They knew who all the players in The System's drama were. Some of them were even neighbors: Charlie Crawford, who ran The System and made his living from bordellos, casinos, and speakeasies, lived with his wife and young daughters on North Rexford Drive in Beverly Hills.

But it wasn't just the physical aesthetics and the philosophical unsavoriness that made those citizens of Beverly Hills opposed to annexation wary of joining Los Angeles. In fact, annexing to Los Angeles was a leap in the dark on both sides of the campaign. For those who wished for Beverly Hills to remain an independent city, the question was where they could obtain water if annexation was voted down. But there were no guarantees that voting to join the City of Los Angeles was going to have a happy, not to mention financially advantageous, ending, either.

In order to finance the herculean task of bringing water from the Owens Valley as well as upgrading the city's infrastructure and services, Los Angeles had voted on and passed a number of bond issues between the years of 1905 and 1922. The first, in 1905, was for $1.5 million; the next, in 1907, was for $23 million. In the years leading up to 1923 there were bonds for electric plants, harbor improvement, fire protection, libraries, and sewage treatment totaling millions and millions of dollars at a time when $1 million equaled just over $14 million in today's money. The total amount of the bond indebtedness of the City of Los Angeles, which was included on Beverly Hills Resolution #73, which called for the election, was almost $84 million. The wording of Resolution #73 was ambiguous; it didn't indicate exactly how much of the outstanding bond debt Beverly Hills would be responsible for. There were good reasons for this fiduciary vagueness. Not only was the proposal to vote for annexation a unilateral action on the part of the Rodeo Land and Water Company, there were no terms or guarantees from the City of Los Angeles to Beverly Hills if the vote ended in favor of annexation. There had been no negotiations between the two cities prior to the annexation vote. In fact, according to the 1909 amendment of Article XXV, Section 257 "Annexation, Consolidation of City and County Governments" of the Los Angeles' civil code, ". . . it shall be lawful, under the charter of the city of Los Angeles, to annex or join to the city of Los Angeles any contiguous city or town in Los Angeles

County, incorporated under the general laws of the State . . . to be governed under the charter of the city of Los Angeles, and the question of annexation or joinder to the City of Los Angeles may be voted upon at an election to be called and held provided by law."[4] Los Angeles did not go out and solicit additional cities and unincorporated territory; the process of annexation had to start in the community that wished to join the larger city. Once a city had voted that it wished to annex, there would be an election in Los Angeles to see if it wanted to annex the other city. Had its vote for annexation been successful, Beverly Hills would not have had any sort of previous agreement in place as to how much of the bond's debt burden it would be expected to assume. Beverly Hills would have had to first wait to see if Los Angeles even wanted it, and then it would find out how much it would cost. The resolution's lack of specificity had the potential to come back and bite Beverly Hills in the pocketbook in a big way, because once Los Angeles voted to annex a city, ". . . the City Council . . . shall also exercise the powers of a Board of Supervisors, including the power to levy and collect taxes, as may be authorized by law, upon all property within such consolidated city and county."[5] A generous interpretation of the terms by Los Angeles could leave Beverly Hills on the hook for a rather large portion of the outstanding debt, at interest rates that ranged between 4 and 6.5 percent per annum. Going forward, if the annexation was approved, property in Beverly Hills would "after such consolidation, be subject to taxation at the same rate with the property in said City of Los Angeles to pay the bonded indebtedness of the City of Los Angeles specified in said petition . . ."[6] not to mention the potential for special assessments levied and fees paid to Los Angeles going forward. To anyone reading the Resolution, it looked as though the Rodeo Land and Water Company was indeed looking at its own self-interest in getting out from under the responsibility of providing water and other services for the City of Beverly Hills, and it wasn't particularly concerned with the debt with which the residents of the city would be saddled for a very, very long time to come. By joining Los Angeles, Beverly Hills might have had to pay dearly for the privilege of receiving water from the Owens Valley.

Aside from the potential financial burden, the residents of Beverly Hills had only to look a few miles east to Hollywood, which had been an independent city between 1903 and 1910, to see examples of what would happen to their concept of a "garden city." Beverly Hills' curvilinear streets, each lined with one type of tree, and expansive lots would probably not survive

City of Los Angeles zoning. Waterfalls on private property? Horses? Independent schools? Probably not. To the celebrity and noncelebrity residents alike, annexation might bring Owens Valley water flowing out of the faucets in their homes, but the costs would include seeing their own private Xanadu fall by the wayside.

Silsby Spalding, the president of the Beverly Hills Board of Trustees at the time of the annexation vote, was opposed to annexation not because of cultural, aesthetic considerations, or the ego-fulfillment of running his own town his way. Spalding believed that independence would be advantageous to Beverly Hills through better public services and a lower tax rate. In the end, giving citizens more bang for their tax buck would help Beverly Hills more than cheap water that would come at a cost of high taxes and having to stand in line to get services from an overextended Los Angeles bureaucracy.[7]

What were the residents supposed to believe? At first many felt that it stood to reason that the Rodeo Land and Water Company was telling the truth about the lack of availability of potable water. It might not be what they wanted, but joining Los Angeles seemed like the only reasonable option. After all, they had to have water.

After Stanley Anderson purloined a copy of the

letter from hydraulic engineer J. B. Lippincott to Burton Green that indicated there was the potential for enough local water for up to thirty thousand residents, he and his fellow prominent citizens of Beverly Hills who were opposed to annexation, with whom he shared its contents, knew the truth. It wasn't so much a lack of available water that was stopping the Rodeo Land and Water Company, but rather a lack of will to spend the money to sink wells and treat the water that was pumped.[8] But Anderson was in a bit of a pickle. He had discovered the Rodeo Land and Water Company's duplicity through chicanery. To widely publicize the letter would cast aspersions on his standing, something he rightfully was not willing to do because, should the Rodeo Land and Water Company prevail in its wish to push through the annexation, Anderson would still have to work with them. According to the transcript of the 1946 conversation, Anderson had originally appropriated the letter in order to hold it over Lippincott, who had agreed, for a fee, to make a number of appearances on behalf of the independence efforts and to say that water was indeed available. Anderson wanted to make sure that Lippincott didn't take a fee from the pro-annexationists and double-cross them by claiming that there wasn't enough water. But how to get the message across to ordinary citizens that annexation to Los Angeles wasn't the only reasonable answer? Even before Lippincott had agreed to appear at community meetings on the subject of obtaining more potable water, there had already been meetings held on the subject, like the one at the Rodeo School where Silsby Spalding had been booed by employees of the Rodeo Land and Water Company. More than $52,000 had been raised at William Joyce's dinner to fund an anti-annexation campaign. That amount would buy plenty of signs and banners for lawns and windows and to hang across intersections, as well as to purchase advertising space, but would signs and meetings be enough? Beverly Hills' prominent anti-annexation citizens such as Stanley Anderson, Silsby Spalding, and William Joyce were personable fellows and well liked in their community. They approached the threat of annexation seriously; Spalding hired a Colonel Sufton, whom Firminger described as "a first class public relations man," while pointing out "[Sufton] did not reside here," to run the anti-annexation campaign. Firminger adds that Beverly Hills resident Frank G. Denison, who worked for Chapman Ice Cream (soon to introduce ice cream parlors in the shape of upside-down cones), was on hand to see to the details. The annexationists were serious as well. Running the campaign was Rodeo Land and Water Company executive Harrison Lewis, the man who had attempted to talk William Joyce over to the pro-annexation side while Silsby Spalding listened, out of sight, in an adjoining room. Lewis was no stranger to attracting attention with publicity stunts: At the nineteenth annual California Real Estate Association meeting held in Santa Ana, California, that concluded on December 9, 1922, Lewis flew in an airplane and personally dropped leaflets on the attendees proclaiming that Beverly Hills was "Los Angeles' most wonderful suburban community."[9]

Had the annexation attempt taken place six years earlier, before World War One, or in another town, the conventional steps of hiring public relations professionals and placing signs and banners on both sides of the issue would have probably been the extent of their efforts. But Beverly Hills in the heady days of the early 1920s was no ordinary town. And while it's true that the anti-annexationists among the city's civic establishment took what they felt was a necessary, albeit conventional, route to a campaign for the cause of remaining independent, they had more ammunition at their disposal than they might have initially been aware of. They had Mary Pickford.

9

Dramatis Personae

———◇◇◇———

There is no contemporaneous documentation that pinpoints exactly when Mary Pickford found out about the proposed annexation of Beverly Hills to Los Angeles, or when she came on board as the leader of the celebrity intervention that would take place to help prevent it. One reasonable scenario is that either Stanley Anderson, a friend of Doug Fairbanks and one of the original organizers of the anti-annexation movement, or Silsby Spalding, also an anti-annexationist who had rented his estate, Grayhall, to Fairbanks in 1918, let the monarchs of Pickfair know what was being planned for their realm. Or perhaps Mary first found out about the annexation from seeing the circulating petition that would bring the question of annexation to Los Angeles to a vote.

It could even have been someone in the pro camp, such as Burton Green or another member of the Rodeo Land and Water Company, who told Pickford.

Regardless of when she found out and from whom, it is safe to say that Mary Pickford decided to oppose the annexation based on her own analysis of the situation. She didn't need men, in positions of authority or otherwise, to make up her mind for her. Mary Pickford, sometimes with the help of her mother, Charlotte, sometimes without, had been more than capable of making decisions without the input of men, who by virtue of their sex and place in the world of business felt they knew best. Mary Pickford determined what was best for Mary Pickford. Once a situation was explained, Mary would filter the facts through her own, and by extension her family's, best self-interest. But why would she care one way or the other if Beverly Hills annexed itself to Los Angeles? For one thing, Mary Pickford was a control freak. In her career, she looked at the revenue streams for the motion picture industry and was one of the first stars to form her own production studio, which not only gave her control of the roles she played, but also control of her fellow cast members, directors, and cinematographers as well as the marketing and advertising. Film distribution was another area where studios helmed by Adolph Zukor and Jesse Lasky made money, for not only did they distribute films produced by their studios, they also distributed films of other production companies as well. Mary, along with her husband Doug Fairbanks, Charlie Chaplin, and D. W. Griffith, founded United Artists to distribute the films their eponymous production companies made. Mary kept a tight rein on her image, and her business acumen was not the public story she wanted to tell. Mary's fans wanted a chaste, forever woman-child and that's what she delivered. She and her studio kept rigid control on how she was depicted in photos: no pens in her hand that could be mistaken for cigarettes and always dressed modestly. She "wrote" a newspaper column extolling old-fashioned values and virtues such as obeying your husband and eschewing gossip. By 1923, the year of the attempted annexation, Mary Pickford would have been a big fish in any pond, but in Beverly Hills, she was a whale. She and Doug ruled the city; they were the magnet that brought bold-faced names to visit them at Pickfair, some of whom liked the neighborhood so much they settled there. The Beverly Hills she lived in was her own creation; she was in charge of the holiday decorations for the city, she and Doug provided funds for the fire brigade. She was a poor girl married to a half-Jew who had worked her way to the pinnacle of Beverly Hills, a new city unencumbered by a Social Register. At this point in her career, she probably had no reason to fear being snubbed by Los Angeles blue bloods, but there were no guarantees that her status as the undisputed queen of the city would carry over after annexation. By her reckoning, filtered through her own self-interest, it was to her advantage to do everything she could to ensure that Beverly Hills remained an independent city. So great was her confidence in herself that it made perfect sense, at least to Mary, that she bring her considerable organizational drive and project management skills to bear.

It was fortunate for the anti-annexation cause that Mary was even available. Beginning with their European honeymoon in the summer of 1920, Mary and Doug had taken long international trips throughout the decade that followed and were often gone for months at a time. In 1921 their travels took them to France, Switzerland, Italy, the Middle East, and Africa; in 1924 they did a three-month whirlwind tour of Europe that stretched from Madrid to Oslo with London, Paris, Copenhagen, Amsterdam, and cities in Switzerland and Germany in between. As it happened, in late 1922 and early 1923 Mary was home, but she and Doug were incredibly busy working, usually on adjoining sets, at their merged studios.[1]

On the other hand, it's entirely possible that Mary looked upon campaigning for the anti-annexationists as not just another chore, but more of a welcome distraction. It wasn't just that Mary was consumed with work, she was consumed with determining the direction that she wanted her work to go. It was a precarious and nerve-racking process and one for which she got little support from her few confidants. To her adoring legions of fans, she was "Little Mary," "America's Sweetheart," but she was also an artist who wanted to grow—as an actor and as a woman, for that matter. Her public had ascribed to her a state of perpetual youth and innocence. They wanted to see her continue to play the roles of children; they wanted Mary Pickford to remain pure in heart and body. Mary Pickford, though, was ready for something else. At the age of thirty, she felt more than a little uncomfortable taking parts that cast her as a preteen; she wanted her roles to grow up. Her mother, Charlotte, who acted as Mary's business manager, might have understood her daughter's desire to break out of the typecasting, but she also understood the bottom line. Mary playing roles such as *Pollyanna* and *Rebecca of Sunnybrook Farm* were guaranteed cash cows, and Charlotte would advise against making any changes. In other words, according to Mama Pickford, if it ain't broke, don't fix it. Mary, though, was interested in exploring her options. Films were still silent, but the artistry that went into their making was light-years ahead of what it had been just ten years previously. Special effects, such as

Mary appearing on-screen simultaneously as two characters—as she did in *Little Lord Fauntleroy*—were becoming more commonplace as the stories being told became more involved. Mary Pickford wanted to stretch creatively and she wanted a director who could help her do that. She wanted Ernst Lubitsch, the famed German director who had helmed *Passion*, a silent masterpiece about the French king Louis XV's mistress set against the backdrop of palace intrigue that was released in the United States in 1920. Period pieces like the 1922 *When Knighthood Was in Flower*, which William Randolph Hearst had bankrolled for his mistress, Marion Davies, were becoming successful vehicles for actresses. Mary thought a sweeping historical drama wrapped in the splendor of royal trappings could be a way to both get what she wanted and still be able to give her audience what *they* wanted. With a period piece in mind, in late 1922 Mary brought Lubitsch to Hollywood to direct her in *Dorothy Vernon of Haddon Hall*, the story of a noblewoman who was a contemporary of Queen Elizabeth I and Mary, Queen of Scots. (It was actually Lubitsch's second foray to the United States. In 1921 Famous Players-Lasky had invited him with much fanfare to work for them. But in the wake of World War One, which had ended in late 1918, there was still enough anti-German sentiment in the air that people were hurling rocks at dachshunds. During his 1921 visit, Lubitsch was on the receiving end of some nasty phone calls and returned to Germany after only a few weeks. Lubitsch's arrival in Hollywood in October 1922 to direct Pickford was decidedly more low key.)[2] Once he was settled and work commenced, the meetings that took place with Mary, her mother, and Lubitsch were fraught. Lubitsch passed on *Dorothy Vernon,* in preparation for which Mary had already spent $250,000 (more than $3.6 million in 2017 dollars). To Lubitsch, Mary suggested *Faust;* she would play the role of Marguerite, the woman who strangles her illegitimate baby. Charlotte would have none of it. For the first time she absolutely forbid Mary from doing a part. *Faust* was shelved and Mary suggested *Rosita,* a story based on a play called *Don Cesar de Bazan,* about an impoverished street singer in Seville, Spain. Lubitsch balked; he didn't think he could work with Mary Pickford. He complained that she wasn't like European actresses. (By this, Lubitsch meant Mary wasn't a steeped-in-drama artiste even when the cameras weren't being cranked.) More wrangling took place and at one point Mary had a private meeting with Lubitsch to remind him that she wasn't just the star of the yet-to-be-chosen movie, but its producer and financial backer as well. Lubitsch threw a tantrum. Mary prevailed.[3] With that sort of drama taking place at work—drama that was *not* in front of the camera where it belonged—Mary just might have looked upon fighting against Beverly Hills annexation to Los Angeles as a palate-cleansing challenge. If she could stand up to just the latest in a long line of cinema auteurs who'd tried to impede her way since the beginning of her career, she couldn't possibly have much to fear from the Rodeo Land and Water Company. (When *Rosita* came out, many of the reviews damned the effort with faint praise. For Mary it may have been a Pyrrhic victory. She proved she could carry a serious picture and appeal to a more sophisticated audience; the cost, though, was losing the audience she already had. Thirty or so years later Mary would write in her autobiography that *Rosita* was "the worst picture, bar none, that I ever made.")[4]

On top of the work and the almost constant entertaining that went on at Pickfair (it's said that the table was set for sixteen every evening to accommodate the acquaintances old and new that Doug invited for dinner), Mary was serious in her charitable commitments. In that winter and spring of 1922 and 1923, she chaired the committee in charge of raising money for the Salvation Army in addition to six other fund-raising campaigns for institutions that cared for "little victims of adversity including two orphanages, one Catholic and one Protestant."[5]

As the saying attributed to Hollywood actress and producer Lucille Ball goes, "If you want something done, ask a busy person to do it. The more things you do, the more you can do." Among the many silver screen stars who had moved to Beverly Hills in the early 1920s, Mary Pickford was the best "get" for the anti-annexationists to help their cause. Pickford and Fairbanks were both dedicated, active participants in the civic life of Beverly Hills after moving in together following their wedding in 1920. In the five years since Doug Fairbanks had treated the fire brigade to dinner after they doused a fire at Grayhall, where he was living, first Doug and then Mary had been generous with their time and money, helping the city procure fire engines and additional equipment, participating in promotions for the Chamber of Commerce, supporting horse shows and horticultural exhibitions, bringing entertainment to the city, and decorating the town every Christmas. It's no secret that both Mary and Doug relished control, although each had her and his own approach. Judging by contemporaneous writings as well as biographies of both, it's likely that the charming and gregarious Douglas Fairbanks would have fared well regardless of which city claimed dominion after the April 1923 election. That's probably not so true for Mary Pickford: She enjoyed being the queen of the city, the boldest of the bold-face names. It was possible she might have had to share that crown, or lose it to someone with just as much money but greater social standing, if and when Los Angeles took over. More importantly, though, Mary saw through the pros and cons of annexation to Los Angeles and realized that because there was no indication of how much of its outstanding bond debt the larger city would saddle on its new addition in the wake of annexation, it had the potential to be a financial disaster for Beverly Hills residents.

Although maintaining her privacy was important to her, Mary Pickford certainly had more reasons for wanting Beverly Hills to remain independent of Los Angeles than fear of intrusion by press and police. From all accounts, Beverly Hills police officer Charlie Blair never had to ask partiers at Pickfair to keep it down, as the goings-on were remarkably sedate. Doug and Mary didn't host any drunken bacchanals. There was no fear of landing in the papers for violating the Volstead Act by getting busted for imbibing wine or spirits: Doug eschewed alcohol even without the incentive of Prohibition. And it was waltzes only, no "jazzes" at the occasional dances. As did most things for Mary, her feelings about annexation ultimately boiled down to money. It's entirely possible that she would have been inclined to view the proposed joining of Beverly Hills to Los Angeles in a more favorable light if there was a financial gain to be had. But after practically inventing how top stars were compensated, and continuing to be one of the young industry's highest-paid actors, who also owned her own production company and was a principal in United Artists, the film distribution company she cofounded, Pickford recognized a bad deal when she saw one. The uncertainty of the terms Beverly Hills would face if it voted to annex to Los Angeles would have struck Pickford as a contractual nonstarter. On hearing an explanation of the proposal, Pickford would have picked up that annexation between the two cities had the potential to be an expensive proposition for Beverly Hills and a windfall for Los Angeles, with the larger city calling the shots. That was not Mary Pickford's idea of a smart way forward for her city.

What Mary needed to do was make sure that message—that Los Angeles would be setting the terms for Beverly Hills to join it—was heard as loud and clear by her neighbors and fellow residents of Beverly Hills as the pro-annexationists' message of "annexation or stagnation," which was delivered courtesy of the signs on lawns, in store windows, and on banners placed across such major intersections as Santa Monica Boulevard and Crescent Drive. But these things needed to be done delicately: Her involvement in campaigning for Beverly Hills to remain independent could not look self-serving. When it came to the local Los Angeles papers, which would be sure to cover the campaign and election, any whiff of elitism could be detrimental. Campaigning for Beverly Hills to remain an independent city could not follow the same playbook as the battles involving her compensation from the studios. In those exchanges Mary had taken the skirmish to the press to curry support from her fans and bring pressure to bear on the studio chiefs. Taking the anti-annexation cause to the press wasn't the right tactic at all. No, for this campaign it wasn't the skills she had honed negotiating with the likes of Adolph Zukor, it was the experience she had gained representing the U.S. government in promoting the sales of Liberty Bonds that would be more in line with what she needed to accomplish. The approach could not look as if her wish that Beverly Hills not join Los Angeles was just a capricious whim, a "let them eat cake" moment of entitled pique. Mary had to deliver the message that she was just another citizen of Beverly Hills.

Once Mary Pickford was on board and lending her considerable skills to the cause, the anti-annexationists had not only her organization abilities and charm, they also had her talent for making her audience *believe*. Mary needed to build common cause within the community between the celebs and non-celebs. Pro-annexationists were hammering home the message that the city's growth was necessary for municipal prosperity and that property values would plummet unless they joined Los Angeles. Mary had to make the citizens of Beverly Hills look beyond the fear that voting against annexation was a vote against their own self-interest. Mary had to counter the fears of her neighbors that voting "no" for annexation would hit Beverly Hills residents in their pocketbooks. In fact it was voting "yes" that could end up costing residents. She made her neighbors aware that since no terms had been agreed to between the cities as to fees and taxes, voting to annex to Los Angeles could end up costing the residents of Beverly Hills plenty through higher taxes, fees, and assessments—and that no one knew how high the price could go. The anti-annexationists needed to make sure the message that there *was* obtainable water in Beverly Hills reached the city's residents, and that the fear that one day soon they would turn on the tap only to find nothing coming out was groundless. Mary needed to reach out to her neighbors and let them know that, as citizens of Beverly Hills, they were all in this together and that remaining an independent city was the smarter course of action for everyone's future.

Both Mary Pickford and Douglas Fairbanks were active in the civic life of Beverly Hills; as individuals, each was also at the heart of emerging movie industry organizations. Mary had founded the Motion Picture

Relief Fund after World War One and Doug was one of the principal organizers of the Academy of Motion Picture Arts and Sciences. But it was Mary, not Doug, who spearheaded the celebrities' campaign against annexation, according to the recollections of those who were there.

It came down to temperament. Although Mary could be high-handed, she had much more of the common touch than Doug—not that the citizens of Beverly Hills, the majority of whom ranged from wealthy to extremely wealthy, fit into the category of hoi polloi. But Doug could be mercurial. He was happy to hobnob with cowboys and stable hands while filming on location, but when he was home he was an inveterate snob, renowned for his infatuation with titles; visiting European aristocracy were often invited to Pickfair. According to an anecdote, Charlie Chaplin called one morning and jokingly asked Doug, "How's the duke?" "What duke?" asked Doug. "Oh, any duke," replied Chaplin.[6] And Mary was, after all, America's Sweetheart. Who better to share news and views with her neighbors than the most famous Girl Next Door of all?

Mary also had great faith in her own abilities to sell an audience, and she understood the power that a great cast could bring to any project. It's in the casting— who was and was *not* part of the anti-annexation troupe—that Mary's strategic fingerprints can be seen the most. Had Doug Fairbanks been pulling together the players for the anti-annexation effort, Charlie Chaplin would have had, if not a starring role, at least a featured cameo. Rudolph Valentino would most certainly not have been included owing to Doug's renowned jealousy. (By her own admission in her autobiographical writings, Mary Pickford had a fraught relationship with Chaplin, her husband's best friend and the couple's business partner in United Artists. And the feeling was mutual; Chaplin thought Mary was talented, but mercenary. As for Rudolph Valentino, Mary recalls in her autobiography that "I never saw Douglas act so fast, and with such painful rudeness, as he did in showing Valentino that he wasn't welcome.")[7]

For this production, though, Pickford pulled out all the stops. Pickford would bring everyone and everything available to the anti-annexation cause: the magnetism of her husband Doug Fairbanks, the sex-appeal sizzle of Rudolph Valentino, the wit of Will Rogers, and the comic relief of Harold Lloyd. Prominent citizens of Beverly Hills who opposed annexation such as Anderson, Spalding, and Joyce had wealth, influence, and regard from those who knew them, Sufton and Denison, the public relations men who were running the more conventional aspects of the campaign, may have had marketing experience, but, collectively, none of them had the instant recognition that fame brought. In any other city that lack of fame might have been a simple fact of life, but in Beverly Hills, celebrity was currency waiting to be invested. Mary Pickford was savvy enough to understand that if it was just her and Doug campaigning to keep Beverly Hills independent it might very well be perceived as a completely selfish, self-serving pursuit. But if she and Doug were joined by a posse of fellow stars, then the optics would suggest that the sentiment against annexation was broader. So, while Mary may have been driving the all-star anti-annexation bus with Doug as her co-pilot, and they could for all intents and purposes have made the journey by themselves, they enlisted six marquee names who were capable, in modern-day parlance, of "opening a picture"—Will Rogers, Harold Lloyd, Conrad Nagel, Fred Niblo, Tom Mix, and Rudolph Valentino—to join up.

The personal styles of the six who joined Mary and Doug in their anti-annexation campaign ran the gamut from extroverted self-promotion and calculated self-interest to outwardly civic altruism to reclusiveness, but they also shared similarities. They had all come from somewhere else to seek fame and fortune in the moving picture business. Some of them were already working in movies when they came to Hollywood. All of them eventually found acting or, it could be said, acting found them. Most became proficient at rearranging the less salubrious bits of their own personal biographies. Most of them had nothing material to lose when they started their careers. All of them became wealthy, although not all of them remained that way. Like Pickford and Fairbanks, Niblo had already shown his support for his town; all the rest of Team Anti-Annexation—except Rudolph Valentino, who would die in 1926—would continue to support Beverly Hills to small and great degrees in the upcoming years. Conrad Nagel and Fred Niblo would also join Fairbanks as founding members of the Academy of Motion Picture Arts and Sciences in 1927.

Harold Lloyd was born in Nebraska in 1893. He moved with his father to San Diego, California, in 1910 after his parents divorced. Within two years, he was acting in comedy one-reelers. In 1913, at the age of twenty, Lloyd moved to Los Angeles and appeared in several Keystone comedies. By 1918, along with his pal and future legendary producer and director Hal Roach, Lloyd began to cultivate his own character, "Glasses," in much the same way Charlie Chaplin created "The Little Tramp." With those round glasses,

Lloyd would become one of the most successful, and richest, comedic actors of the silent film era, with earnings that would rival Pickford's, Fairbank's, and Chaplin's.

Interestingly, while Harold Lloyd had bought the land bordering Benedict Canyon and, according to his granddaughter, Sue Lloyd, installed his mother in a small dwelling on the property, as of 1923 Lloyd himself hadn't taken up residence there. His magnificent home, Greenacres, complete with a waterfall and a meandering creek, was in the planning stages at the time of proposed annexation. But like Pickford and Fairbanks, he understood the value privacy and exclusivity would have in the future. He understood that in a city with such a small population, those with fame—and the wealth and notoriety that accompanied it—could expect their wishes to be given greater consideration. Beverly Hills would be amenable if they wanted to build a waterfall or keep horses on their property; Los Angeles had rules against keeping horses in the better neighborhoods. Not to mention the small police force that turned a blind eye to parties where liquor bottles, shoes, and undergarments were found on the lawn the morning after the festivities.

Fighting to stop the annexation movement was Lloyd's first civic involvement in the city that would be his home until his death in 1971, but it would be far from his last. Lloyd was one of the supporters of the iconic Electric Fountain, which features the statue of a Native American praying while waters illuminated by colored lights dance around it. The fountain, located at the intersection of Wilshire and Santa Monica boulevards, anchors the west end of Beverly Gardens Park, the greensward that runs the length of the portion of Santa Monica Boulevard contained within Beverly Hills. Lloyd also played a less positive role in the city. In the early 1940s, when black actors and businessmen expressed interest in moving to Beverly Hills, he joined a neighborhood association whose goal was to enforce the city's restrictive covenants that prohibited nonwhites, which included Jews, from buying or renting property in the city. The action was dismissed in federal court; in 1948 the Supreme Court would rule that restrictive covenants based on race could not be enforced.

It's not an overstatement to say that Tom Mix, born in 1880 in Mix Run, Pennsylvania, invented the celluloid cowboy hero archetype who is clean-cut and always saves the day, and along with it, the Western. He got his start after getting a job as a cowboy at the Miller Brothers 101 Ranch in Oklahoma and appearing in its Wild West Show. Mix wielded enough clout in the early days of Hollywood that not only was Fox Film Corporation paying him $7,500 a week, but it also built "Mixville," a twelve-acre indoor-outdoor set on the grounds of the Edendale lot located in what is now the Echo Park neighborhood of Los Angeles.

Mix was an addition to the team that would have pleased both Mary Pickford and Doug Fairbanks. Like Doug, Tom Mix was a man's man, full of bravado and nerve. Also like Doug Fairbanks, Mix did most of his own stunts. (For a long time Mix claimed he did *all* of his own stunts, but there were a few instances where stunt doubles were used.)

Mix and Fairbanks would have parted ways, however, when it came to Mix's fondness for drink. (In March 1924, Tom Mix had an altercation with his wife Victoria Forde, the facts of which differ greatly depending on the teller of the story. But the end of the story is not in doubt: Victoria shot her husband in the arm, the bullet finally lodged next to Mix's spine, and alcohol was involved. No one was arrested and the facts of the case were hushed up by the studios for almost ten years.)[8]

As someone who had almost no formal education within the walls of a schoolroom, Mary would have appreciated Mix's voracious reading. Journalist, novelist, and screenwriter Adela Rogers St. Johns, who wrote screenplays for Mix, admired the cowboy actor for reading the entirety of Shakespeare's plays because he felt he should. The two would discuss the Bard's works and St. Johns felt Mix's take on the plays was "enthusiastic and well reasoned."[9]

Perhaps most importantly for the anti-annexation cause, Mix had an instinctive feel for branding—literally. Mix had his brand, TM, set at an angle and surrounded by a diamond shape,[10] imbedded in the tires of his cars so the impression could be readily seen on the many unpaved roads in the Los Angeles area. He also hung a giant "TM" in neon lights above his Beverly Hills mansion. The over-the-topness of Mix's self-promotion was certainly not in the same wheelhouse as Mary's more circumspect approach to fame, but she must have recognized its value to the cause. Tom Mix burned bright in the local consciousness and there have always been people who are attracted to flamboyant displays. Mary knew that sort of flamboyance would work to the cause's advantage.

Will Rogers, the other cowboy of the group, and Beverly Hills are inexorably linked, even though he moved to his Pacific Palisades ranch in the late 1920s. He was the honorary mayor of Beverly Hills, a position that afforded him the opportunity for countless self-deprecating jabs. Rogers helped with publicity for the city's real estate companies; the Polo Lounge at the Beverly Hills Hotel took its name by virtue of the fact that Rogers and his polo-playing buddies used it as a post-match watering hole; and the park just south of the hotel, where Sunset Boulevard and North Beverly and North Canon drives intersect, was named for him in 1952. Starting in 1922, the year before the annexation vote, until his death in 1935, long after he had moved from the city itself, it would be Will Rogers, as much as anyone, who would help raise the city's profile by using Beverly Hills as the dateline on his syndicated column.

Rogers, part Cherokee on both sides of his family, was born in Cherokee Nation, Indian Territory, which would become Oklahoma, to an upper-middle-class family in 1879. After trying—and failing—to become a cowboy on the Argentinian pampas, Rogers decamped to post–Boer War South Africa, where he worked on a ranch in Natal province. After doing rope tricks in an Australian circus, Rogers returned to the United States and worked the vaudeville circuit, eventually ending up in New York City. He was lured to Hollywood in 1918 to ply his wrangling skills in silent films, a bit ironic considering his performances in the *Ziegfeld Follies* were a combination of cowboy rope tricks and wry political observation. Will Rogers could *talk*. He was witty and came off as a likable, wholesome, sensible family man who never took himself or the trappings of wealth too seriously. It was a rare individual who did not fall under his charming spell, which was exactly what Mary was counting on.

Director Fred Niblo also hailed from the state of Nebraska. He was born Frederick Liedtke in 1874, adopting the stage name Fred Niblo when he began performing in vaudeville. He took a break from performing when he married George M. Cohan's older sister, Josephine, and began managing the Four Cohans. Niblo's film career began 1912 in Australia.

After Josephine's death in 1916, Niblo moved to Hollywood, where his directorial career took off. He directed Douglas Fairbanks in two of his biggest films, *The Mark of Zorro* and *The Three Musketeers*. Niblo also directed Rudolph Valentino in *Blood and Sand*. Niblo is perhaps best known, however, as being the principal director of *Ben-Hur*, which became the third-highest-grossing silent film of all time.

Although not as famous to the general public as the rest of the anti-annexation team, Fred Niblo was a wise choice for the task at hand. As one of the first stars of the silver screen to move to Beverly Hills, taking up residence not long after the city incorporated, he was well known to his fellow residents. Even more in his favor, perhaps, his civic commitment predates Pickford and Fairbanks': Niblo, along with actor Charles Ray, and local real estate developers and businessmen, formed a company to create a community store in the commercial district of Beverly Hills during World War One.

Conrad Nagel, like Will Rogers, came from an upper-middle-class home in the Midwest. In Nagel's case, his father was dean of the Highland Park College Music Conservatory in Des Moines, Iowa, and his mother was a locally renowned singer. After graduating from college, Nagel decided to try his luck in the new medium of moving pictures. Studio executives were sold on his all-American appeal, his six-foot-one-inch height, and his wholesome Midwestern good looks. He was smart and well organized and liked living in Beverly Hills. The depth of his pro–Beverly Hills feelings would come to the fore a few years after the annexation vote, when he would head a movement to build a wall around Beverly Hills to keep the outer world at bay.[11] Doug Fairbanks would join Nagel in the effort to build the wall around Beverly Hills.

If there was a dark horse on Team Anti-Annexation, it was Rudolph Valentino. It's safe to assume that it was Mary who asked him to join the effort, because Doug Fairbanks was extremely possessive of Mary and jealous of even the most cursory attention paid to her by any man, let alone the 1920s equivalent of the sexiest man alive. The thought that Valentino might so much as look at Mary, let alone speak to her privately, would be enough to send Doug into a fury. But Mary knew what she was doing. In 1923 Valentino, who was an intensely private and sensitive man who had endured his share of innuendo and scandal, including suggestions of homosexuality and an arrest for bigamy before *The Four Horsemen of the Apocalypse* and *The Sheik* made him a household name, was one of the biggest stars there was. It didn't matter to Mary that Valentino hadn't even settled in Beverly Hills yet—he bought Falcon Lair, his estate in Beverly Hills, after the annexation vote. Mary realized that it was his desire for privacy that would motivate him to sacrifice it for a short time to help the anti-annexation cause. That, and she also knew that Rudolph Valentino had something the other seven, who were also at the absolute pinnacles of their careers, did not: time.

In late 1922 and early 1923, Valentino was on a "one-man strike," as he told the press, against the Famous Players studio to whom he was under contract. At the time he was making $1,250 a week with a promise of an increase to $3,000 a week in the following three years. It may have been a fortune at a time when the average annual earnings for an American household were $2,000, but Valentino pointed out that Mary Pickford had been earning $10,000 a week in 1916. While his contract was in dispute, Valentino couldn't work in motion pictures. With free time on his hands and the promise of an independent city to call home in the near future, Valentino even agreed to a photo op of a door-to-door canvass in the campaign against annexation.

This then was the force of celebrity, and the power of it dawned on Mary Pickford. Who wouldn't open the door to Valentino? Or any of the other seven campaigning against annexation, for that matter? Instantly recognizable, defining what these eight had as "a head start" in forwarding a cause doesn't come close to explaining how they were able to penetrate even the wealthiest and most exclusive of enclaves. The wealthy and the well connected succumbed to movie star dazzle as readily as factory workers; celebrity seemed to transcend any boundary.

10

Playing with Fire

———◆◇◆———

I t took a big story to catch the reading attention of the citizenry of Los Angeles in the early 1920s. On any given day there were at least six papers covering the news of the comings and goings—including engagements, nuptials, and divorces—of the moving picture stars, Volstead Act scofflaws, the arrests of bigamists, and traffic accidents involving women drivers. Not to mention the frenzied, continuing coverage of the pursuit of Clara Phillips—dubbed the Tiger Woman—who in late 1922 had murdered a rival for her husband's affections with a hammer purchased at a local five-and-dime, had been arrested, escaped from the county jail, and was being pursued by the Los Angeles County Sheriff all the way to a hideout in the jungles of Honduras.[1]

In the early part of the twentieth century bombs were often the weapon of choice for those who took violent exception to a government policy. And newspapers were among the targets. On October 1, 1910, union activist brothers John J. and James B. McNamara placed a suitcase packed with sixteen sticks of dynamite and equipped with a faulty timer in an alley next to the *Los Angeles Times* building. Because the bomb went off at one a.m. instead of four a.m., when the building was supposed to be empty, twenty-one *Times* employees were killed and more than a hundred were injured. While the bomb itself wouldn't have been able to bring down the substantial building located at Broadway and First Street, it was placed over a gas main and the resulting explosion and fire were catastrophic. The blast rocked downtown Los Angeles and its metaphorical reverberations were felt for decades. It was the fieriest and costliest battle between union organizers and Harrison Gray Otis, the adamantly anti-union publisher of the paper, and one of the deadliest acts of terrorism in the early part of the twentieth century. But long after the reason the McNamara brothers, who eventually pled guilty to the charges, had bombed the *Times* faded from memory, the impact of the explosion on the psyche of the city remained. Even in 1923—thirteen years later—in Los

Angeles, bombs at newspapers were taken seriously. They caught, and kept, the city's attention.

(The subsequent 1911 trial of the brothers, who were represented by Clarence Darrow, was dubbed "the trial of the century," replacing the Leopold and Loeb "trial of the century" that had taken place in Chicago in 1904. There wouldn't be another "trial of the century" until Roscoe Arbuckle's three trials for manslaughter in San Francisco in 1922.)

It wasn't the turbulent era's only bomb. Anarchists had set off a bomb on July 22, 1916, during a parade in San Francisco for Preparedness Day, proclaimed in anticipation of America's entry into World War One. That bomb killed ten and injured forty, and the same anarchists were purportedly responsible for a black powder bomb set off in Milwaukee, Wisconsin, in 1917 that killed nine policemen. And then an explosion went off that cut wealthy capitalists, including many of Beverly Hills' most prominent citizens, to the quick. On September 16, 1920, a bomb carried in a horse-drawn wagon parked across the street from the headquarters of the J.P. Morgan Bank on Wall Street exploded. It killed thirty people outright, with another eight dying of injuries sustained in the blast, and more than a hundred and forty individuals were seriously hurt. After the blast, trading was halted on

the New York Stock Exchange to forestall panic selling, but in the haste to clean up and get the exchange
open for business the next day, practically all of the
evidence was destroyed or seriously compromised. Investigators were flummoxed—initially because, as
there was a fair amount of construction going on in
the area, they thought the explosion might have been
an accident. That theory was eliminated when flyers
were found at a nearby post office with the ominous
message: "Remember we will not tolerate any longer.
Free the political prisoners or it will be sure death for
all of you. [Signed] American Anarchist Fighters." The
era's forces of evil—at least according to capitalists
and law enforcement—organized labor, anarchists,
and Communists were afoot in the land and they were
delivering bombs. The investigation into the Wall
Street bombing would remain active for more than
three years and there would be occasional updates in
the newspapers.

So a bomb exploding in Beverly Hills at its weekly
newspaper's offices in the early days of the annexation
campaign was an alarming turn of events, to say the
least. With approximately one thousand generally
well-heeled inhabitants that included famous film
stars, studio moguls, business titans, and the head of
The System, L.A.'s crime syndicate, Beverly Hills was
a small town populated with big egos. No one was on

the fence when it came to the issue of annexation to Los Angeles, but at most the back and forth between those against and those in favor of joining the bigger city had been a vigorous war of words, as befitted a city populated with wealthy, educated citizens. There were signs in shop windows, placards on lawns, banners spanning major intersections, meetings at homes and at the Beverly Hills Hotel, meet-and-greets with autograph signings by celebrities, and editorials in the local paper both for and against. Behind the scenes there was certainly scheming, along the lines of Stanley Anderson appropriating the letter from the office of hydraulic engineer J. B. Lippincott that clearly indicated the Rodeo Land and Water Company was not telling citizens the whole story when it came to available water resources. But in spite of the fact that almost everyone had at least a long gun in their homes to deal with marauding coyotes and to dispatch injured wildlife, nothing had driven the citizens of Beverly Hills, or their neighbors in Los Angeles, for that matter, to violence over this issue.

That is, until February 26, when the "Infernal Machine," as the press referred to the bomb, exploded in the hands of pro-annexation Al Murphy, the editor-publisher of the *Beverly Hills News*. Accompanying the device was a chilling note: "The Hour at Which You Must Make the Decision Has Arrived. Lay

Off the Annexation Stuff. Our Next Move Will Be T.N.T." It was signed: K.K.K. And, purportedly, it wasn't the first explosive device that had been deployed in response to the annexation proposal. Clark Fogg, senior forensic specialist of the Beverly Hills Police Department, recalls retired Beverly Hills police officers telling him of another bomb that had been planted at the Beverly Hills Civic Center, which hadn't exploded, before the one that had detonated at the offices of the *Beverly Hills News*.[2]

This shocking turn of events rocked the community and beyond. Even accounting for clandestine maneuverings between members of the city government and representatives of the Rodeo Land and Water Company on the question of who would supply the city's water, the annexation was not being handled as a backroom deal with no public input. A petition requesting a special election to settle the question of annexation had been circulated and was days from being presented to the Board of Trustees of the City of Beverly Hills when the bomb exploded.

In 1923 the medium of radio was still in its infancy, especially as a disseminator of news. To get the attention of the community, the region, the nation, and the world, an event had to make the papers, the more the better. In the case of the *Beverly Hills News* bomber, if the goal was to attract attention, he, she, or they got their wish. News of the explosion was covered in five of the Los Angeles daily papers: the *Los Angeles Times, Los Angeles Record, Los Angeles Evening Herald, Los Angeles Evening Express,* and *Los Angeles Examiner.* Over the next few days the story of the bombing was picked up and printed in papers across the country—it would appear as a small item on the front page, above the fold, of the *New York Times* on March 1, 1923—bringing attention to what had been a rather mundane political interaction between two cities at the western edge of the United States. Suddenly, the battle for Beverly Hills had taken an ugly turn and the whole country knew about it.

Beverly Hills News editor Al Murphy, who despite some reporting to the contrary, received only superficial burns to his hands when he triggered the device, took his fifteen minutes of fame seriously and went to town giving quotes to any reporter of a Los Angeles daily paper who would listen. The splashiest coverage by far came from William Randolph Hearst's *Los Angeles Examiner,* where the explosion made the front page on February 27, 1923, in the over-the-top reporting that was the signature style for a Hearst newspaper. The coverage was full of drama and hyperbole. Murphy's most copious quotes were in the *Examiner,* where he declared that he was the target because of his personal and, through his paper, professional stand in favor of annexation. "I have received numerous threats, both by telephone and unsigned letters, in the past few weeks, but this machine is the first actual attempt to do me bodily harm. I have armed myself and am ready for their next move," Murphy proclaimed to the *Examiner* reporter.[3] Murphy also stated that he had taken what was left of the bomb to Los Angeles sheriff William I. Traeger to check for fingerprints and that he gave the sheriff "the names of the parties whom he strongly suspects of being responsible." The *Los Angeles Evening Express* reported that suspects had been named and there would be little difficulty in bringing "the guilty parties to justice."[4] The *Los Angeles Record* went as far as reporting that the persons who planted the bomb had "attempted to kill Al Murphy, Beverly Hills editor, by means of an infernal machine,"[5] which was a big leap from Murphy's own assertion that the bomber wished to injure him.

Considerable attention was paid by newspapers to descriptions of the actual device in addition to quoting the message that was attached. An almost full-page photo of what was left of the bomb, including the message, dominated the front page of the February 27, 1923, *Los Angeles Examiner*. In the *Examiner*, Murphy describes the package that contained the "infernal machine" as being "wrapped in manila paper, and a number of canceled postage stamps to lend the appearance that it had been through the 'mails,' were attached." Murphy went on to add that he thought "it was a present from a friend" and that he attached no suspicion to the box.[6] In the *Los Angeles Evening Herald* the bomb was described as "composed of two dry cell batteries and a complicated system of switches which ignited a quantity of black powder when the cover was lifted."[7] The *Los Angeles Record* offered a similar description in its February 28, 1923, edition, adding that the wiring system "was capable of exploding a large amount of high explosives."[8]

Sheriff Traeger had a lot on his plate in February 1923, what with the Tiger Woman on the loose in Central America (L.A. County undersheriff Eugene W. Biscailuz deputized his wife before the couple headed down to Honduras to supervise the capture of Clara Phillips. Mrs. Biscailuz would contract malaria while in the jungle, dying from it in 1950) and a jail corruption scandal of deputies taking bribes for releasing inmates. Nevertheless, Traeger assigned two L.A. sheriff's deputies, John B. Fox and Charles Catlin, to investigate.[9]

According to the February 27, 1923, edition of the *Los Angeles Evening Express,* in addition to the law enforcement investigation, the "direction of the search for the culprits is in the hands of R. J. Culver, president of the Culver Corporation."[10] The *Los Angeles Evening*

Express also reported that prominent residents of Beverly Hills made sure "unlimited money has been made available" to discover the guilty party or parties. In the same article, Mr. Culver is quoted as saying "that there are now working on the case a number of detectives from the Burns agency and the force of Sheriff Traeger." (The Burns Agency was founded by William John Burns, the American "Sherlock Holmes," who is famous for conducting a private investigation into the notorious steeped-in-anti-Semitism wrongful conviction of Leo Frank in the 1913 murder of Mary Phagan in Atlanta. Burns' investigation showed that Frank was innocent of the crime. Not that it did much good. When Frank's death sentence was commuted to life in prison by the governor of Georgia in 1915, a mob abducted Frank from the penitentiary and lynched him. Burns had also investigated the *L.A. Times* bombing in 1911 and served as a director of the Bureau of Investigation, the predecessor to the FBI.)[11] Not to be outdone, the *L.A. Times* reported that $500 had been sent to the paper as a reward for information leading to the arrest of the person or persons who sent the bomb. The source of the reward was not reported.

A follow-up article in the *Los Angeles Examiner* reported that the day after the bombing "hundreds thronged the office of the News to receive confirmation from Mr. Murphy of the explosion."[12] In the same article, one unnamed Beverly Hills resident said of the bombing, "That's not the spirit of Beverly Hills." Murphy, his hands and face still sporting bandages from the burns he had sustained the previous morning, agreed with the sentiment expressed by the resident who was quoted and then went on to deliver what can only be described as one of the most confusing statements of the whole confusing situation: "Although I have been bitterly assailed for the stand taken in my newspaper in favor of annexation, I do not regard the bomb as the work of Beverly Hills people who are honest in their convictions on the opposite side of the issue."[13] Which raises the question: Who else but someone who had something to either gain or lose would take such extreme action? Was Murphy suggesting that for some unknown reason outside agitators were interfering with a legal political process in a small suburb on the western edge of Los Angeles? It's highly unlikely that any of the usual suspects of the era who tended to resort to bombs, such as Bolsheviks or anarchists, had wandered into the small, affluent community determined to save it from itself by preventing its annexation to a larger city. Who else but residents of Beverly Hills cared whether or not their city voted to annex itself to Los Angeles? The answer, of course, is no one. (As for the list of suspects Al Murphy had given to the Los Angeles Sheriff's

Department, those names are lost to the mists of time. In 1969 the L.A. County Sheriff's office purged its records when the filing system was changed. Before that purge, the department saved every piece of paper going back to the 1850s. As Michael A. Fratantoni, the archivist for the Los Angeles County Sheriff's Department, wrote in an email, "What a treasure that must have been.")[14]

L.A. sheriff deputies Fox and Catlin pursued the investigation from two diverging angles suggested by the Beverly Hills citizens they interviewed: that the bomb truly was the work of anti-annexationists, and from the diametrically opposite position that it was a publicity stunt to garner sympathy for the pro-annexation effort in general and Editor Murphy in particular.

No one, including those on Mr. Murphy's list of potential suspects, was ever arrested for the bombing. In fact, Deputies Fox and Catlin determined there had never actually been a bombing. On March 1, 1923, two Los Angeles dailies, the *Evening Herald* and the *Record*, reported that the explosion had not been a bomb after all. The *Los Angeles Evening Herald* reported that "what was first believed to be an attempt to assassinate Al Murphy, editor of the *Beverly Hills News*, was classed today by deputy sheriffs who investigated the case as a practical joke. . . . The officers found the 'bomb' was made out of small firecrackers."[15] The *Los Angeles Record* reported that the "joke" had been played on Murphy by a resident "in connection with the annexation fight."[16] The whole story was digested and reduced to a two-paragraph summary on the front page of the *New York Times,* also on March 1, whose headline, " 'Infernal Machine' Explodes; Firecrackers Injure Editor," and description of the damage as "the blistering of [Editor Al] Murphy's hand"[17] offered a succinct summary of the whole bizarre incident. As for the *Los Angeles Examiner,* after its follow-up articles on the pursuit of suspects, expectation of arrests, and the rally in support of Al Murphy and against the "bomb," there wasn't another drop of ink devoted to the subject.

Naturally, there was a great deal of speculation about who had sent the so-called bomb. Considering the distance from scandal and negative publicity the celebrities living in Beverly Hills wanted to maintain, it's difficult to imagine that any of them would have taken an action that would result in even more scrutiny. In fact, it's safe to say that most of the celebrities associated with the anti-annexation movement would not have been amused by either the explosion, joke or otherwise, or the insinuation that it had been sent by a resident. Actors and film crews alike developed a healthy respect for flammable and explosive material, because as fun as it looked, in reality, making movies was dangerous work. Aside from film stock, which was made from highly flammable silver nitrate that regularly burst into flames at studios, causing both severe injuries and substantial property loss, actors themselves were frequently at risk. Explosives were often used as special effects, especially in location shooting, and accidents that sometimes caused serious injuries were not uncommon. In November 1923, six months after the annexation election, Tom Mix was almost killed in a stunt-gone-wrong that was staged during the filming of *Eyes of the Forest*—an explosive charge planted under the path he was riding on went off prematurely. In August 1919, at the cusp of his becoming a star, Harold Lloyd wasn't even making a movie when a bomb—originally made to cause an explosion in a non-Lloyd film—blew the thumb and forefinger off his right hand and blinded him for a time. Lloyd had been shooting publicity stills, one of which was to show him lighting a cigarette from the lit fuse of what was supposed to be a papier-mâché bomb. Only it wasn't pretend, it was a real explosive that had for some unknown reason been placed with bomb facsimiles. Lloyd spent six weeks in the hospital, and while his sight returned, in an era before antibiotics doctors feared that if gangrene developed on his hand, the wound might kill him.

Truth be told, though, Mr. Murphy's paper wasn't held in the highest regards in the community. Because the bomb hadn't been very powerful, gossip of the day suggested that it had been self-directed to make the pro-annexation cause more sympathetic to the citizens of Beverly Hills. In notes on a history of Beverly Hills he was writing for the *Beverly Hills Citizen* in 1941 about the annexation attempt, former city clerk B. J. Firminger wrote: "There was a paper here then called *Beverly Hills News*. The columns were, of course, for sale. The publisher sided with the annexationists which was a splendid thing for the other side—it being *that* sort of paper." In the May 9, 1941, *Beverly Hills Citizen* article, Firminger modified what he'd written to suggest that Al Murphy was driven by economic need, writing, "The publisher was living from hand to mouth, and the columns of the paper were apparently for sale."[18]

In fact, every step of the march toward potential annexation to Los Angeles had been recorded on the public record. The petition requesting a special election so the citizens of Beverly Hills could vote on the matter had been circulated early in 1923 and had received enough signatures to be presented. And at the March 1, 1923, meeting of the Board of Trustees of the City of Beverly Hills presided over by Silsby Spalding, a motion to accept the signed petition to the fully attended Board "asking for an election to be held to decide on the annexation of the City of Beverly Hills to Los Angeles was presented."[19] Eleven days later, on March 12, 1923, the Board of Trustees swore in Beverly Hills city clerk John G. Soulay, who testified "that he had checked all the signatures with the original registration certificates and found that the petition was signed by 376 qualified registered voters."[20] Soulay's testimony also included the fact that there had been "slight irregularities" in twenty-seven signatures. Soulay's final conclusion was that the 349 correct and authentic signatures represented more than 25 percent of the 703 registered voters in the city. After City Clerk Soulay completed his testimony, the Board of Trustees swore in the Beverly Hills city attorney, who testified that the petition was correct in form. In light of the legitimacy of the petition, the Board of Trustees adopted Resolution #73, calling for a special election to settle the question of whether the cities of Beverly Hills and Los Angeles shall be consolidated. Resolution #73 passed unanimously by the four trustees in attendance for that meeting. The vote, to be held at the Beverly Hills Civic Center, was scheduled for April 24, 1923. For the four successive weeks preceding the election, a notice that included the names of the cities proposed for consolidation (Beverly Hills and Los Angeles), the date of the election, the voting precincts, and the polling place would be printed in the *Beverly Hills News*, "a weekly newspaper of general circulation in said City of Beverly Hills, and hereby designated as the newspaper in which said notice shall be published."[21]

The firecracker "bomb" sent to Al Murphy wasn't the end of the publicity stunts or dirty tricks that preceded the actual election. There would be at least one more zinger pulled on the morning of April 23, 1923, the day before the election. But there would not be any more explosions. Whether or not the bomb had been an ill-conceived ploy to drum up support for the annexation cause, saner heads prevailed going forward. Beverly Hills did not exist in a vacuum. Governments around the world were still reeling from the effects of the Bolshevik Revolution in Russia and the tactics used during Ireland's fight for independence from England. Acts of terrorism, which is what the incident was considered at first, made law enforcement agencies sit up and take notice. Labels like "revolutionary" accompanied things like "infernal machines" and bombs. It's a label that's hard to imagine anyone on either side of the annexation issue in a community of wealth and fame would want.

Al Murphy and the *Beverly Hills News* didn't last long after the "practical joke." Within a year of acting as the newspaper of record for the election, the paper ceased operations and slipped into an oblivion so deep that not only is there no digital record of its existence, actual hard copies are for all practical purposes non-existent as well. (The Special Collections division at the Beverly Hills Library has only one.) Al Murphy folded his tents, as it were, and slipped off into the metaphorical night. There are no records of him as a journalist after the mid-1920s. The city's next weekly, *The Beverly Hills Citizen*, began publication in April 1923, about the same time the vote for annexation was taking place.

11

On Their Own

———◇◇———

A s the dust settled in the aftermath of the Infernal
Machine/box of firecrackers' detonation at the offices of the *Beverly Hills News,* Mary Pickford and
her team of anti-annexationists got to work. Regardless
of how much planning went into the endeavor, their
efforts had to come off as low key and grass roots, not
calculated and certainly not in the public eye. Mary
Pickford, Douglas Fairbanks, Will Rogers, Tom Mix,
Fred Niblo, Conrad Nagel, Harold Lloyd, and Rudolph
Valentino had to be laser focused on the voters in
Beverly Hills. The gatherings they would hold, which
included picnics, meet-and-greets, photo ops, autograph sessions, and door-to-door canvassing, were not
for fans, they were created for *neighbors.* While it
was quite common for the daily papers to print

announcements provided by the studios highlighting the public comings and goings of movie stars, Mary and her group's work on behalf of keeping Beverly Hills independent from Los Angeles largely stayed out of the papers. Judging by the skill Mary Pickford had shown in manipulating the press throughout her career, the assumption can only be that this was how she wanted it. In fact, the only stories we have of the anti-annexation efforts by the Beverly Hills Eight are anecdotes from their fellow citizens.

The famous picture folk may have been successful at keeping their efforts on behalf of Beverly Hills' independence out of the papers for the most part, but that didn't mean that their personal and professional lives didn't continue to be the subject of relentless media attention. On January 28, 1923, just as the campaign for the annexation vote was getting under way, the *Los Angeles Times* ran "Marry in Haste, and Repent in the Courtroom," a multipage article by Myrtle Gebhart that tracked in detail the ever-changing marital status of picture folk, and how those gyrations impacted the moviegoing public. In the article, Gebhart writes:

"Really the man or the woman, whatever be his special line, who is successful in getting into the limelight professionally, oftentimes seems to have a penchant for attracting the spotlight quite as readily to his private affairs.

"The film stars suffer particularly. Their art is national in appeal. Whatever concerns their personal affairs also has a big national significance. They are known everywhere personally, intimately, through their work on the screen. The stories of their matings or mismatings are featured with almost equal prominence in New York and Oshkosh. The news concerning them is always the sensation of the hour.

"Glancing over records of a few years back I discover that Mildred Harris was then Mrs. Charles Chaplin and that Mary Pickford answered to 'Mrs. Owen Moore.' Owen is now married to Kathryn Perry. Doug [Fairbanks], now Mister Mary, then had another wife, a non-professional.

"That Mary Pickford's marital unhappiness with Owen Moore was instrumental in developing her great talent I do not believe, for hers is one of those God-given geniuses that depend upon no extraneous force but grow within themselves to flower. But certain evidences of her marriage with Doug are to be seen—in the swagger with which Little Lord Fauntleroy pranced across the screen, wherein surely Doug's influence was disclosed."

The article was accompanied by an almost full-page

illustration by *L.A. Times* cartoonist A. Zetterburg, who signed his work "Zett," of a castle atop a steep mountain—that bore more than a passing resemblance to Pickfair—with the "Marital Happiness" at the lofty summit and the word "Divorce" placed at strategic points on the way up the craggy side and a roiling audience of moviegoers at the bottom.[1]

It was exactly the kind of hometown paper coverage that Mary Pickford worked arduously to avoid. Obviously, she wasn't always successful.

It wasn't just about keeping their private lives out of the media glare; a low profile in the media on the part of the stars campaigning against annexation was a good idea all around. The stars participating in the anti-annexation movement wanted to keep their outreach as one-on-one, as up-close-and-personal as possible. After their experiences rallying for Liberty Bonds during World War One, Mary Pickford and Doug Fairbanks knew better than anyone how crowds at their personal appearances could grow exponentially and get out of hand. Unlike raising money for the war effort, campaigning against annexation to Los Angeles didn't need a critical mass; it only needed the attention of the one thousand or so Beverly Hills residents of voting age. After all, it wasn't money for Liberty Bonds that Mary and her team were trading access to themselves for, it was votes. Not only that, when it came to the press, the last thing any of the eight celebrities wanted was for the combined words "anti-annexation" and "bomb" used in a newspaper article to be associated with them.

Naturally, it was William Randolph Hearst's *Los Angeles Examiner* that managed to get a few digs in about the rich and famous who lived in Beverly Hills, casting the election as a rather frivolous exercise of the leisure class that had little better to do. (The paper had a conflicted approach to the moneyed suburb. Even though it cast itself as the voice of the people, Hearst's mistress, actress Marion Davies, had one of the palatial mansions—paid for and maintained by Hearst—that the paper so loved to pillory.) The *Examiner*'s article is headlined "Plain Water Stirs Beverly," and it tells of a fund-raising effort by the anti-annexationists that raised $32,000 in about four minutes before naming some of the more illustrious non-celeb and celeb "antis": "among the [no-to-LA] are such plethoric individuals as Frederick K. Stearns, multimillionaire pharmaceutical manufacturer; S.M. Spalding, with a car for every mood; J.K. Woolwine, brother of the District Attorney, and a host of other celebrities, which includes such hill dwellers as Charlie Chaplin, Douglas Fairbanks, Charles Ray, Fred Niblo and Will Rogers.

"The town is plastered with red-type rejoinders,

data, charges, counter-charges and a great deal of other naked language, the latest on the boards being a large sheet hurtling this: 'Lie No. 1.' "[2]

There are no records indicating exactly how the city fathers felt about the involvement of the moving picture folk, only anecdotal asides in notes for articles and in the transcript of the 1946 conversation with onetime owner of the Beverly Hills Hotel, Stanley Anderson. It's a good guess, though, that those who were against the annexation welcomed the support of their famous neighbors and those in favor of joining Los Angeles chafed at what looked like the outsized influence of the picture folk.

But it is the involvement of the picture folk and their influence that changed the equation; this political campaign differed from any that had taken place previously anywhere else in the world. Both sides had hired marketing and publicity men, so there were certainly plenty of the more conventional approaches that had stood the test of time for informing and trying to influence the electorate one way or another. Aside from the external trappings of any election, such as signs and banners, there were plenty of informational meetings, mostly at the city's schools, with experts that included hydraulic engineers, the city's Board of Trustees—as officials of the civic government were called—representatives of the Rodeo Land and Water Company, developers, and realtors.

It was all in the presentation. By any measure, especially wealth, the citizenry of Beverly Hills was sophisticated for its time. They took the issue of deciding on annexation seriously, were engaged in the campaign, and were interested in learning everything they could about the impact it would have on their city. But the meetings with experts and elected officials were just that, meetings—where a man, or men— would address and take questions from citizens in an audience. Each armed with their own set of facts that fit their arguments, these were the experts— technocrats, bureaucrats, and businessmen—who could speak knowledgeably about water tables, wells, purification plants, land values, density, transportation, and schools. There was no doubt that the men who campaigned both for and against felt they had the best interests of the city and its denizens at heart. Since most of the men were successful in their chosen fields, they were often very convincing when they spoke. Informational gatherings on the challenges Beverly Hills was facing were elucidating, but in a thoroughly conventional, expected way.

So what was it that made Mary Pickford think she, and by extension her team of fellow picture folk, could step in and change the calculus of an election process and influence voters? Well, for one thing, from her experience promoting Liberty Bonds she had a pretty good idea how instant recognition owing to her fame could be channeled into influence. But in the Liberty Bond tours, she was exhorting the crowds to channel their better selves and support the war effort; in Beverly Hills she would be convincing her neighbors to join her in taking a leap of faith. For most canvassers for a cause, the first step in the process would be introducing themselves and trying to get a foot in the door to make their case. That's not something Mary Pickford and the other seven celebs had to do. When you have one of the world's most famous faces, introductions are redundant; if you show up at a neighbor's front door, it's a foregone conclusion that you're going to be invited in. While it was true that Mary and her cohorts were not experts in the nuts and bolts of city services such as water, trash collection, and sewage treatment, that wasn't the platform they were campaigning on. It was their belief that cities were not just places that existed in geography, they were *ideas*, and that was the object of their crusade to remain independent.[3] Los Angeles was one idea: that water meant might and might meant right. In little over fifteen years, fueled first by the anticipation of and then by the reality of the melted snowpack that streamed down from the eastern slope of the Sierra Nevada Mountains through the Owens Valley, and then by the petroleum being sucked from under the ground, Los Angeles had become a megalomaniacal steamroller subsuming the cities that stood in line waiting to be absorbed. The independent city of Hollywood had been an idea; a teetotal town with ruler-straight streets lined with pepper trees and a church on every corner. For all the promises that Los Angeles made in 1910 to Hollywood, a city founded by those who eschewed alcohol, after Hollywood voted for annexation and Los Angeles had voted to accept its annexation, none of those assurances had been kept. Quite likely, with the same instincts that had served Mary her entire life, she intuited that things would go the same way for Beverly Hills. The garden city with its large lots on curvilinear streets, each bordered by a single kind of tree, and a permanent greensward adjacent to Santa Monica Boulevard, on the length that ran through Beverly Hills, created to forever separate the residential and business districts, would not stand. Los Angeles had its own way of doing "city" and it involved businesses on main streets, such as Santa Monica Boulevard, and cheek-by-jowl housing packed on the straight streets that bisected the commercial streets at right angles. Eventually, and judging by the changes the independent city of Hollywood underwent fairly quickly after annexation, what had made Beverly Hills unique would be lost. For the campaign for Beverly Hills to remain an independent city, Mary would have to create a different approach. That may just have been the secret sauce that Mary Pickford figured out and put to use: making the leap between connecting with an audience and making a personal, often one-on-one, live-and-in-person connection with her neighbors. She and her fellow anti-annexationist picture folk were actors, familiar with assuming roles and making audiences believe. They were perfectly capable of shifting their performances depending on the role and the intended audience. Experts could give opinions to the citizens of Beverly Hills in an effort to make them see the respective sides, but since making others suspend disbelief was their stock-in-trade, by making themselves available up close and in person, Mary and her cohorts could make the same citizens *believe*. It worked because people felt as though they knew and trusted Mary Pickford, Douglas Fairbanks, Tom Mix, Harold Lloyd, Will Rogers, Conrad Nagel, Rudolph Valentino, and Fred Niblo—and actually had a personal relationship with them through their roles in the movies. Mary Pickford, Doug Fairbanks, and the rest of the team capitalized on that illusion and had only to establish the common denominator of a shared hometown to make a connection that would resonate and matter. And by going door-to-door,[4] that's exactly what they did. All it cost was time on the part of the picture folk, but the value of their time and effort in convincing their Beverly Hills neighbors to vote against annexation was priceless. Residents of other cities who were opposed to annexation to Los Angeles, including Hollywood and Venice, hadn't had celebrities to aid their cause.

Of the two sides, the anti-annexationists certainly had more reason for concern about the outcome. The issue of adequate water for Beverly Hills, and where additional sources would be found, was front and center. The legal process being brought by the pro-annexationists contesting the quality of the additional water source that Beverly Hills had found was moving forward in Sacramento, the state capital, with its first hearing set for April 7, 1923. Both sides realized that, depending on the rulings of the California State Board of Health, the timing for the hearings was either propitious or calamitous. However, the anti-annexationists felt they had the most to lose. If the Board of Health determined the water was unsafe so close to the election, that message might mean the death knell for Beverly Hills. In the absence of a ruling, and with the attention of Beverly Hills citizens fixed on the machinations that were taking place in front of the California State Board of Health in

Sacramento in the days leading up to the special election on Tuesday, April 24, 1923, their work was necessary.

According to the minutes of the first meeting before the State Board of Health in Sacramento on April 7, 1923, with both representatives of the Rodeo Land and Water Company's Beverly Hills Utility Company, City Engineer A. J. Salisbury, and trustee and attorney Paul E. Schwab from the City of Beverly Hills in attendance, the City of Beverly Hills requested a permit to develop a well water supply and a permit for sewage disposal. No decisions on the quality of water from the new well were made. According to the minutes of the meeting, the motion was carried and a public hearing was scheduled for nine o'clock in the morning, April 20, 1923, at the Pacific Finance Building in Los Angeles.[5] Because the hearing in Los Angeles was scheduled four days before the vote, the outcome had the potential to deliver the election to one side or the other. The stakes could not have been higher.

Although there are no minutes of the April 20, 1923, meeting held in Los Angeles, the proceedings were covered by two of the city's daily papers, the *Los Angeles Examiner* and the *Los Angeles Times*. And according to the *Examiner*, there were fireworks coming from both sides. Given the timing, the hearing gave the pro-annexation advocates the opportunity for a preemptive move: If the trustees of the City of Beverly Hills' petition for the authority to install a water supply system was turned down, the vote on annexation the following Tuesday would certainly go in favor of joining Los Angeles. After all, Beverly Hills had to have water. To that end, pro-annexation advocates, with their doctors, scientists, and lawyers in tow, showed up in force to do what they could to stop the process. The anti-annexationists had come prepared with their own team of experts that included attorney and city trustee Paul E. Schwab along with City Engineer A. J. Salisbury, both of whom attended the first meeting in Sacramento, along with attorney Major Walter Tuller and J. B. Lippincott (the hydraulic engineer who had worked for both sides of the annexation issue and was now on the anti-annexation payroll). Representing the pro-annexation cause was Francis J. Heney, hired by the Rodeo Land and Water Company as their chief council for the effort. Heney was assisted by H. F. Prince as well as engineers A. L. Sonderegger and E. R. Bowen.

Both sides of the annexation argument lined up to testify before Dr. Walter M. Dickie, the secretary of the California State Board of Health; Chief Engineer F. R. Goudrey of the southern division; and attorney J. M. McFarland. Each side spoke about the quality of water from the Gold Seal Well, the name of the potential new water source for Beverly Hills, in what was seen as a battle by proxy for the election that was to take place the following week. According to coverage in the *Los Angeles Examiner*, "Dr. C.G. Griffin of a local chemical company filed a report at the hearing in which he condemned the water from the well as unfit for human consumption and domestic purposes. He said the mineral matter made it too hard for laundry, cooking, bathing and other domestic purposes, and unfit to drink."[6] The health expert for the anti-annexation side, Dr. Walter Brem, countered that the mineral content made the water "the kind a health resort might like to use."[7]

The key witness of the proceeding was C. G. Gillespie, the California State Board of Health's sanitary engineer. In his testimony, Gillespie said that the Gold Seal Well "might be safe if it were drilled deep enough with two iron pipes, one inside, the other with a concrete filling between." But there was a caveat, according to Gillespie, "the well, after being drilled to 150 feet, might not produce enough water to bother about." At that, the anti-annexationist lawyers pounced, saying that "the proceedings were of a political rather than an inquisitory nature, and that the main purpose was to sway voters at the annexation election which Beverly Hills will hold next Tuesday."[8]

And so it went. Sensing that the matter had as much or more to do with politics than the safety of Beverly Hills' future water supply, the Board of Health adjourned and postponed further consideration, along with their decision on issuing a permit to drill the new well, until its next regular meeting, which would be in May—after the annexation election. At the end of its coverage of the April 20 hearing, the *Los Angeles Examiner* wrote, "Should annexation to Los Angeles be voted at next Tuesday's election the whole controversy will end, as Beverly Hills will get Owens River aqueduct water, and the disputed wells will not be needed."[9] While the pro-annexationists had been unable to stop consideration for a permit being issued, they must have been quite pleased by the article's conclusion; they couldn't have said it better themselves.

No doubt the Beverly Hills Eight worked feverishly over the weekend to counter the *L.A. Examiner* news article that appeared the Saturday before the election. Then, on Monday, April 23, 1923, the day before Beverly Hills voters were to go to the polls, the pro-annexationists sprang their final pre-election stunt. Bottles containing water with a high and quite odoriferous sulfur content were placed on every doorstep with a note that said, "Warning! Drink Sparingly of This Water, As It Has Laxative Qualities," followed by this all-capital-letter admonition: "THIS IS A SAM-PLE OF THE WATER WHICH THE TRUSTEES OF THE CITY OF BEVERLY HILLS PROPOSE AS A WATER SUPPLY FOR OUR CITY!" The label con-cluded with the official-sounding, "An Affidavit cer-tifying that this water is a true sample taken from the well the trustees propose is deposited at the First National Bank of Beverly Hills."[10] Bottles of smelly water were piddling accomplishments for Harrison Lewis, the Rodeo Land and Water Company em-ployee who was in charge of the pro-annexation campaign. Lewis had been the Rodeo Land and Water Company employee who had tried to turn anti-annexationist William Joyce to the pro-annexation side and he was well known for attention-getting pub-licity stunts. According to reports in the *Los Angeles Record,* the previous December, Lewis had "person-ally superintended the printer's ink bombing" ex-horting development in Beverly Hills by dropping flyers from the open cockpit of an airplane on the attendees of the California Real Estate Convention that took place in Anaheim.[11]

According to recollections of former city clerk Firminger, judging by the signage displayed on homes and businesses, the general feeling in Beverly Hills was distinctly anti-annexation. But that could be an example of twenty-twenty hindsight on his part; when it comes to the outcome of an election, looks can be deceiving. None of the anti-annexationists, famous silent screen stars and prominent wealthy citizens alike, would have gone to bed the night before the election confident of victory.

Tuesday, April 24, 1923, dawned cool and clear, if a bit on the damp side, with a relative humidity of seventy-five percent. The forecast from the local office of the U.S. Weather Service printed in the *Los Angeles Times* that morning was for continued clear skies, no precipitation, and a high intraday temperature of 67°F,[12] perfect conditions for going to the polls. At last, as B. J. Firminger wrote, "The shouting and tumult, the arguing and buttonholeing [*sic*] ended, the day of the great annexation election finally arrived."[13] According to the *Examiner*, "The campaign . . . was one of the most spectacular ever staged in California. It is estimated that the two sides spent something like $75,000, which is about $75 a voter."[14]

By the terms set forward in Resolution #73, the polling place, located at the city clerk's office at City Hall on Canon Drive near Burton Way, was to be opened at six a.m. and stay open until seven p.m. For the purposes of the special election, "one special election precinct is hereby created . . . and shall embrace all of the territory within the said City of Beverly Hills."[15]

As usual, it was the coverage in the *Los Angeles Examiner* that was the most colorful. In its April 25, 1923, edition it wrote:

"The motion picture stars who have helped to make the hills of this suburban Elysium blossom with their palatial piles nearly all voted early, and they did not overlook the very practical requisite of loading their cars down with an interesting miscellany of maid servants, chauffeurs, gardeners, chefs and what not. The sentiment among these, it was reported, was unanimously against annexation. Among the names to go into the register during the early morning watches were those of Priscilla Dean, Enid Bennett, Gloria Swanson, Mr. and Mrs. Charles Ray, Douglas McLean, Fred K. Niblo, Hobart Bosworth and Robert McKim."[16]

According to former Beverly Hills city clerk Firminger, about 90 percent of the city's registered voters went to the polling place that day[17] in what was "said to be the largest vote ever recorded in a single Los Angeles county precinct."[18] The atmosphere was tense, to say the least. Francis J. Heney, the San Francisco lawyer hired by the pro-annexation Rodeo Land and Water Company, was in attendance "with law book in hand, seated where he could look the electorate in the face."[19] In fact, according to the April 25, 1923, *L.A. Examiner* article, "The room was full of challengers and every citizen had to run a gauntlet of the codes and statutes appertaining: it was enough to make the most honest sovereign voter shudder with a sense of guilt to find all these suspicious eyes boring him through."[20]

In contemporaneous press reports and Mr. Firminger's 1941 article, the exact tallies vary by a few votes. According to the *Examiner* and the *Times,* there were 489 votes against and 326 votes in favor of annexation, with 32 votes declared invalid. Firminger's article put the totals as 507 against and 337 in favor. Regardless, percentage-wise the "no's" had it by a healthy 33 percent margin. Still, in absolute numbers, only 170 or so votes prevented Beverly Hills from becoming part of Los Angeles. Only 170 votes meant success instead of failure for the "battle of the real estate interests that sponsored the annexation idea, against the motion picture people who have chosen Beverly Hills as their home. . . ."[21]

The intense scrutiny of the poll watchers on both sides meant the vote tally took quite a while and it was late before the results were announced, but once the defeat of annexation was proclaimed the town cut loose in ways it had never done before, or since, for that matter. Victory was celebrated with torchlight parades, police and fire sirens, car horns, and a marching brass band playing "There'll Be a Hot Time in the Old Town Tonight."[22] In Firminger's account "pandemonium broke loose. All rules were suspended by common consent,"[23] meaning that corks were popping and spirits were flowing freely in open defiance of Prohibition. Otherwise staid citizens, including Beverly Hills City Trustee Norman Pabst, "commandeered the fire engine and had it driven up one street and down the other."[24] Steve Glassell, who had been one of the few real estate agents opposed to annexation at a meeting of the realty board in late 1922, passed out signs with "Glassell voted NO!" printed on them.[25] In the heat of the moment, some sore winners among the anti-annexationists acted out: "Hose lines were connected to fire hydrants near homes of those who had favored consolidation and, amid the sounding of horns and the ringing of the [fire] bell, water was turned on the lawns. Reactions of the besieged were varied. One who took the whole thing too seriously appeared at his front door with a shotgun."[26] One of the lawns flooded was that of Burton Green, the largest shareholder of the Rodeo Land and Water Company, according to the recollection of Paul E. Schwab.[27]

The celebrations continued at private homes, and Pierce Benedict indicates in his 1934 history that there was a celebratory party on May 11, 1923, but he unfortunately neglected to provide a guest list. There is no record of Mary Pickford or any member of the Beverly Hills Eight attending any of the celebrations either the night of the election or in the days after. Like Mary and Doug, most members of the Beverly Hills Eight would remain involved in the civic affairs of Beverly Hills for years to come. In the late 1950s, as the only surviving members of the Beverly Hills Eight, Mary Pickford and Harold Lloyd would be members of the Committee for Honoring Motion Picture Stars, the organization responsible for the memorial sculpture dedicated to the Beverly Hills Eight.

Not so much for the larger-than-life Tom Mix. His time in Beverly Hills would not extend much beyond the fight against annexation; Mix would move away from the city not long after he was shot by his wife in 1924 at their home. Even without the unfortunate gunplay, Mix's restless nature predisposed him to being peripatetic, moving from studio to studio, seeking ever higher paychecks. One of his most famous salary disputes was with Joseph P. Kennedy during Kennedy's tenure at FBO pictures. Of Kennedy, Mix said, he was a "tight-assed, money-crazy son-of-a-bitch."[28] Eventually his high living, multiple ex-wives, and the Depression would bankrupt Mix, who died in a traffic accident in Arizona in 1940. Mix's cowboy archetype would be an inspiration, however, to future stars including Marion Morrison, who would become John Wayne, and actor-turned-politician Ronald Reagan.

It's impossible to know exactly what course Rudolph Valentino's life would have taken. He was interested in every aspect of filmmaking, including directing. Valentino was also keen to own a vineyard, according to Frances Marion. He moved into Falcon Lair, his Beverly Hills estate, in 1925; in August 1926, Valentino died after complications from surgery for gastric ulcers and appendicitis.

While Mary Pickford would continue to remain active in the civic affairs of Beverly Hills until her death, the fight against annexation was a one-and-done when it came to her direct political involvement. Which was very much in keeping with Mary's philosophy of looking forward. No doubt, the challenge of saving Beverly Hills from annexation having been accomplished, Mary was on to her next task. She had movies to star in and produce; an eponymous studio and a distribution company, United Artists, to run; charities, including the Motion Picture Relief Fund that she organized after World War One, to support; and the Academy of Motion Picture Arts and Sciences to help found with her husband and Conrad Nagel, among others.

Now that Mary Pickford had helped prevent the annexation of Beverly Hills to Los Angeles, the details of moving forward as an independent city were left to the men who ran it. According to B. J. Firminger's account in the *Beverly Hills Citizen,* as well as the notes on his manuscript, Beverly Hills was fortunate to have the trustees they had. Firminger sings the praises of Silsby Spalding, the president of the Board of Trustees of the City of Beverly Hills, who eventually became mayor in 1928. It was Spalding, aided by many others, including Paul Schwab and Norman Pabst, and supported by the findings of the engineering firm of Salisbury, Bradshaw and Taylor, who put forth a $400,000 bond measure later in the same year annexation was voted down. The bond was to take care of securing new water sources, as well as paying the $250,000 to purchase the Beverly Hills Utility Company, the price of which was determined by the California Railroad Commission, the predecessor to the state's Public Utilities Commission. After all was said and done, the Railroad Commission determined a purchase price for the utility service that had been set up by the Rodeo Land and Water Company. Had that been done immediately, it would have settled the issue without the threat of annexation. Firminger wrote about the kerfuffle, "Perhaps, however, the struggle made a better town. Smooth seas do not make good sailors."[29] It was an expensive sailing lesson.

As she had done in so many other areas of her chosen career, Mary Pickford had been the first to navigate the unknown territory between celebrity and politics. She may have moved aside after accomplishing her political goal, leaving others to finish the job, but every journey begins with a first step, and it was Mary Pickford who took it. She had realized that having one of the most famous faces and recognizable names in the country could be an effective guiding light and a magic key that instantly opens doors that might otherwise be shut forever. Succeeding generations of stars with political goals took it from there. And judging by their accomplishments in being elected to the highest offices in the United States government, it's a lesson that has been learned well by those who followed her in fame.

Afterword

It probably didn't occur to her at the time, but what Mary Pickford set in motion by enlisting her team of picture folk A-listers to campaign for a political cause, in this case against Beverly Hills' annexation to Los Angeles, was nothing short of revolutionary. It doesn't spoil the end of the story to say it worked: Beverly Hills remains an independent city now in its second century.

In 1923 the idea that film stars could interfere in places like politics, where only men of serious mien had gone before, was fresh and new. In all likelihood the more hidebound political operatives who were aware of what had happened in Beverly Hills, California—and there can't have been many—would have been tempted to dismiss the whole endeavor as a one-off. They could tell themselves that now that the rich, spoiled stars of the silver screen who had wanted a city to themselves had attained their goal, they would flounce off back to the land of make-believe from whence they came. Oh sure, in times of national emergency, like World War One, the government could call on film stars to do their bit raising money and morale, but for all intents and purposes, that would be it. After being of use, the men in power fully expected the famous actors and actresses to respectfully step away from the political stage and return to the soundstage.

Needless to say, the stars didn't do that. Between the years of 1916 or so, when the first actors and actresses began to get billing on the flickers, and 1923, the year of the annexation battle, the more prescient of that first wave of stars who had achieved fame and fortune realized that it was possible to also have political power. After World War One, the mutual seduction between celebrity and politics was on. Although it flew under the radar, increasingly the exposure celebrities offered began to be noticed by politicians and political parties. During the presidential election of 1920, candidate Warren G. Harding hobnobbed with studio heads and film stars, each circling the other to see how best to further their interests. Calvin Coolidge, who became president upon Harding's death in 1923, was enamored of radio and film technology. Coolidge became the first president to appear in a film with accompanying sound. Local Southern California politicians crossed paths both socially and commercially with studio executives and stars on an almost daily basis. Other alliances between politics and Hollywood that would bear fruit in the future were also being forged. Joseph P. Kennedy, a producer with FBO Pictures in the 1920s, was carrying on a not-so-secret affair with Gloria Swanson. In those halcyon days of early Hollywood, with then up-and-coming Swanson on his arm, Kennedy met *everyone*. His sons would not only follow in his footsteps when it came to celebrity associations, they would outrun him. His granddaughter Maria Shriver would marry action-hero actor Arnold Schwarzenegger, who would mastermind a recall of a sitting governor of California before running for and winning the seat for himself.

Had Mary Pickford and her blockbuster cast of anti-annexationists' foray into political action failed, had the vote in Beverly Hills ended in favor of annexation instead of against it, the entire celebrity-political equation might have evolved quite differently. (Not to mention, a city that looms large in the world's collective imagination would not exist.) If the biggest stars of the day couldn't come together in 1923 and sway enough of their neighbors to see a situation their way, would there even have been any subsequent celebrity interventions in politics? Would stars, even those like Ronald Reagan, who was president of the powerful Screen Actors Guild, contemplate calling on their equally illustrious peers to help them make the leap into mainstream local, regional, and eventually national politics?

Mary and the rest of the Beverly Hills Eight's aim was to make politics work for them, and the methodology they developed was a success. In her approach to the fight against Beverly Hills' annexation by granting access, limited as it might be, to herself and fellow celebrities, Mary Pickford wrote the first handbook for direct celebrity involvement in nonindustry political maneuvering. The next step was to transition this newfound influence on politicians into assuming the actual *roles* of politicians. It happened faster than most might think: In 1926, Will Rogers was named honorary mayor of Beverly Hills, and in light of his career as a columnist and lecturer who never shied away from expressing political opinions, it's completely reasonable to assume he might have pursued elected office had he not died in an aviation accident in 1935. Helen Gahagan Douglas, who starred in one movie and married popular actor Melvyn Douglas, began her political career in the 1930s and was elected to Congress in 1944, serving until 1951.

She may have lost her Senate race to Richard Nixon in 1960 (John F. Kennedy contributed to his fellow congressman, Nixon, in his battle against Douglas), but she exacted some small revenge by slapping the man who would eventually have to resign the presidency with the sobriquet "Tricky Dick." The clever nickname was for naught, though. After painting the Democrat Douglas as sympathetic to the Soviet Union, Nixon won California's Senate seat in a landslide. Next up from the silver screen in politics was George Murphy in a run for the Senate in 1964. Murphy probably came to the nation's attention in the wake of Tom Lehrer's satirical—and staggeringly politically incorrect—song written in 1965, "George Murphy," whose concluding lyrics were "Yes, now that he's a Senator, he's really got the chance / To give the public a song and dance!"

Lehrer and America may have been amused at thinking Murphy was a lightweight soft-shoeing it across Capitol Hill, but Murphy came to politics in much the same way the future president Ronald Reagan did: as president of the Screen Actors Guild. That experience, plus Murphy's instant name recognition, gave him the edge. It would offer Reagan the same advantage in his campaign for governor of California and president of the United States. Everyone already knew who they were; there was no need to slog in the political trenches that usually started with city council or school board seats for either of them.

In the case of the Beverly Hills Eight's stand against annexation, it was about furthering their own agenda and preserving the independence of their city. Whether it was independence of the schools, a separate police force, or maintaining a garden-like setting, the celebrities who campaigned at Mary's side sought and found common cause with their neighbors in their opposition to annexation. While many of Beverly Hills' wealthy residents must have valued the insulation of living in a small city with its own small, compliant police force, that was adjacent to, but not actually part of, Los Angeles, none cherished it as much as the stars. The eight who came together to fight annexation didn't broadcast that their agenda was primarily to maintain their privacy. Luck, timing, and talent had brought them to Beverly Hills, where they had discovered a refuge from a world that was very much with them all of the time. And while none of the rising stars bemoaned their fame, all felt the scrutiny, and because they were all famous—and flawed—they looked for ways to shield themselves from overzealous coverage. With at least six daily newspapers in Los Angeles alone, what the stars did, where they went, and with whom was covered relentlessly, becoming daily fodder for the broadsheets.

That pursuit of individual agendas is a constant theme in the continuing forays into politics by celebrities. Ronald Reagan, who had been a Democrat, was so put off by the perceived infiltration of Communist influence in Hollywood it drove him to change political parties and to pursue higher and higher elected offices. Sonny Bono, frustrated by bureaucracy in attempting to open a restaurant in Palm Springs, ran for mayor of the desert city—and won. He eventually ran for and won a seat in Congress. The bill Bono is associated with is named for him: the Sonny Bono Copyright Extension Act, which extends copyright protection by twenty years to, for example, songwriters such as himself. (The legislation's derisive nickname is "The Mickey Mouse Protection Act.") Other entertainers-turned-politicians such as Al Franken had long been self-proclaimed "policy wonks." But who really needed any sort of actual political experience? Arnold Schwarzenegger had been a big-screen action hero and was married to a Kennedy. How hard could it be to be governor of California, the most populous state in the United States? There are two parts to this equation, though. Voters in the United States imbue celebrities with expertise by virtue of their fame alone. Thus imbued, with millions of people putting their faith and hopes in them, celebrities seem more than comfortable assuming the mantle of leadership. Bolstered by fans who believed that the Donald Trump they saw on television was a capable and experienced leader, it's entirely plausible that he saw little difference between a reality TV show, with its big "reveal" at the end, and a run for the American presidency. Certainly Trump, who had no experience whatsoever—unlike Reagan, who had been politically active during his career as an actor before running for office and serving two terms as California's governor, or Fred Thompson, senator from Tennessee, who had been minority counsel on the Senate Watergate Committee as well as an actual prosecutor before he played one on TV in *Law & Order*—used his name recognition as a means to an end. There may have been bumps on the road, but fame was the vehicle that conveyed Trump directly to 1600 Pennsylvania Avenue, Washington, D.C. It's impossible to say just what Mary Pickford would have made of the intersection of politics and celebrity in the second decade of the twenty-first century. Because she firmly believed in using fame to her advantage in getting what she wanted, chances are good that she would not have had any problems with it whatsoever.

Regardless, when Mary Pickford got involved in the political process and took a stand against Beverly Hills' annexation almost one hundred years ago, she is the one who started paving Donald Trump's road to the White House.

Notes

Chapter 1: Rancho Rodeo de las Aguas and the Invention of Beverly Hills

1. Pierce E. Benedict and Don Kennedy, *History of Beverly Hills* (Beverly Hills, CA: A. H. Cawston and H. M. Meier, 1934).

2. "Communications," in Donald S. Frazier, ed., *The United States and Mexico at War* (New York: Macmillan Reference Books, 1997).

3. Irving Stone, "Beverly Hills." Original Drafts and Final Copy of Article Published in *Holiday*, October 1952. Courtesy of The Beverly Hills Library Historical Collection.

4. "Treaty of Guadalupe Hidalgo," by Richard Griswold del Castillo, in *The United States and Mexico at War*, ed. Donald S. Frazier (New York: Macmillan Reference Books, 1997).

5. Ibid.

6. Benedict and Kennedy, *History of Beverly Hills.*

7. Les Standiford, *Water to the Angels: William Mulholland, His Monumental Aqueduct, and the Rise of Los Angeles* (New York: HarperCollins, 2015).

8. Michael Gross, *Unreal Estate: Money, Ambition and the Lust for Land in Los Angeles* (New York: Broadway Books, 2011).

9. Ibid.

10. Ibid.

11. Robert S. Anderson with Victoria Kastner, *The Beverly Hills Hotel: The First 100 Years* (Beverly Hills, CA: The Beverly Hills Collection, 2012).

Chapter 2: The Beverly Hills Hotel and the Birth of Its Namesake City

1. Elmer Grey, F.A.I.A, "Vicissitudes of a Young Architect," *The Architect and the Engineer,* January 1933.

2. Ibid.

3. Genevieve Davis, *Beverly Hills: An Illustrated History,* produced in cooperation with the Beverly Hills Historical Society (Northridge, CA: Windsor Publications, 1988).

4. Pierce E. Benedict and Don Kennedy, *History of Beverly Hills* (Beverly Hills, CA: A. H. Cawston and H. M. Meier, 1934).

5. Ibid.

6. Michael Gross, *Unreal Estate: Money, Ambition and the Lust for Land in Los Angeles* (New York: Broadway Books, 2011).

7. Ibid.

Chapter 3: Setting the Stage

1. Neal Gabler, *An Empire of Their Own: How the Jews Invented Hollywood* (New York: Crown Publisher, 1988).

2. Mary Pickford, "My Whole Life: $10,000 a week at 23 . . . then—Douglas Fairbanks," *McCall's Magazine,* 1954.

3. Gregory Paul Williams, *The Story of Hollywood: An Illustrated History* (Los Angeles: BL Press LLC, 2011).

4. Ibid.

5. Ibid.

6. Ibid.

7. Cari Beauchamp, *My First Time in Hollywood: An Anthology* (Los Angeles: Asahina & Wallace, Los Angeles, 2015).

8. Eileen Whitfield, *Pickford: The Woman Who Made Hollywood* (Lexington: University Press of Kentucky, 1997).

9. Tracey Goessel, *The First King of Hollywood: The Life of Douglas Fairbanks* (Chicago: Chicago Review Press, 2016).

Chapter 4: A Crash Course in Influence

1. James R. Mock and Cedric Larson, *Words That Won the War: How the Creel Committee on Public Information Mobilized American Opinion Toward Winning the World War* (Princeton, NJ: Princeton University Press, 1939).
2. Ibid.
3. Gregory Paul Williams, *The Story of Hollywood: An Illustrated History* (Los Angeles: BL Press LLC, 2011).
4. Mock and Larson, *Words That Won the War*.
5. Eileen Whitfield, *Pickford: The Woman Who Made Hollywood* (Lexington: University Press of Kentucky, 1997).
6. Ibid.
7. Mary Pickford, *Sunshine and Shadow* (Garden City, NY: Doubleday & Company, 1955).
8. *New York Evening-World*, April 13, 1918, From the collection of the Mary Pickford Foundation, AMPAS.
9. Pickford, *Sunshine and Shadow*.
10. Ibid.
11. Tracey Goessel, *The First King of Hollywood: The Life of Douglas Fairbanks* (Chicago: Chicago Review Press, 2016).
12. Ibid.
13. Ibid.
14. Ibid.

Chapter 5: *Veni, Vidi, Vici*

1. Marc Wanamaker, *Early Beverly Hills* (Charleston, SC: Arcadia Publishing, 2005).
2. Tracey Goessel, *The First King of Hollywood: The Life of Douglas Fairbanks* (Chicago: Chicago Review Press, 2016).
3. Peggy Dymond Leavey, *Mary Pickford: Canada's Silent Siren, America's Sweetheart* (Toronto: Dundurn, 2012).
4. Ibid.
5. Goessel, *The First King of Hollywood*.
6. Ibid.
7. Ibid.

8. Kevin Starr, *Inventing the Dream: California Through the Progressive Era* (New York: Oxford University Press, 1985).

9. Ibid.

10. Eileen Whitfield, *Pickford: The Woman Who Made Hollywood* (Lexington: University Press of Kentucky, 1997).

Chapter 6: The War Against Hollywood and the Lasting Legacy of Bad Behavior

1. Kevin Starr, *Inventing the Dream: California Through the Progressive Era* (New York: Oxford University Press, 1985).

2. Ibid.

3. "How You Gonna Keep 'em Down on the Farm (After They've Seen Paree')," music by Walter Donaldson, words by Joe Young and Sam M. Lewis. Published by Waterson, Berlin & Snyder Co., New York 1919.

4. William J. Mann, *Tinseltown: Murder, Morphine and Madness at the Dawn of Hollywood* (New York: HarperCollins, 2014).

5. Frances Marion, *Off with Their Heads!: A Serio-Comic Tale of Hollywood* (New York: The Macmillan Company, 1972).

6. Mary Pickford, *Sunshine and Shadow* (Garden City, NY: Doubleday & Company, 1955).

7. Mann, *Tinseltown: Murder, Morphine and Madness at the Dawn of Hollywood*.

8. Ibid.

9. Ibid.

10. Ibid.

11. Ibid.

Chapter 7: Meanwhile, in Beverly Hills . . .

1. *"Daily NewsLife*—Beverly Hills, Calif., Extracts from notes taken from Paul E. Schwab," B. J. Firminger, Retired City Clerk of Beverly Hills, 1954. Courtesy of the Beverly Hills Library Special Collections.

2. Ibid.

3. "Beverly Is Stirred Up by Petition," *Los Angeles Times*, April 21, 1923.

4. "A Discussion of the Early History of Beverly Hills," transcript of a conversation among Lawrence Block, Ben Hoy, Ivan Traucht, Arthur Pillsbury, Stanley Anderson, and Claude Kimball, April 19, 1946. Courtesy of Robert S. Anderson.

5. Ibid.

6. Pierce E. Benedict and Don Kennedy, *History of Beverly Hills* (Beverly Hills, CA: A. H. Cawston and H. M. Meier, 1934).

7. Ibid.

8. Letters of B. J. Firminger, volume 1-F, courtesy of the Beverly Hills Library Special Collection.

9. Ibid.

10. "Beverly Water Supply Up," *Los Angeles Times*, November 25, 1922.

11. Ibid.

12. Les Standiford, *Water to the Angels* (New York: HarperCollins, 2015).

13. Ibid.

14. Ibid.

15. Ibid.

16. Ibid.

17. Ibid.

18. Marc Wanamaker, *Early Beverly Hills* (Charleston, SC: Arcadia Publishing, 2005).

19. "A Discussion of the Early History of Beverly Hills," transcript of a conversation among Lawrence Block, Ben Hoy, Ivan Traucht, Arthur Pillsbury, Stanley Anderson, and Claude Kimball, April 19, 1946. Courtesy of Robert S. Anderson.

20. Frances Marion, *Off with Their Heads! A Serio-Comic Tale of Hollywood* (New York: The Macmillian Company, 1972).

21. Ibid.

22. Ibid.

23. Ibid.

24. Ibid.

25. Ibid.

Chapter 8: "California's Floating Kidney Transplanted from the Midwest"

1. Frances Marion, *Off with Their Heads!: A Serio-Comic Tale of Hollywood* (New York: The Macmillan Company, 1972).
2. Ibid.
3. Richard Rayner, *A Bright and Guilty Place: Murder, Corruption, and L.A.'s Scandalous Coming of Age* (New York: Doubleday, 2009).
4. Civil Code of the City of Los Angeles, pages 206–207. www.lacity .org/your-government/government-information/city-charter -rules-and-codes
5. Ibid.
6. City of Beverly Hills Resolution #73, signed by John G. Soulay, City Clerk of the City of Beverly Hills.
7. B. J. Firminger, "Annexation Battle in 1923," notes for *Daily News-Life*, April 1954. Courtesy of the Beverly Hills Library Special Collection.
8. "A Discussion of the Early History of Beverly Hills," transcript of a conversation among Lawrence Block, Ben Hoy, Ivan Traucht, Arthur Pillsbury, Stanley Anderson, and Claude Kimball, April 19, 1946. Courtesy of Robert S. Anderson.
9. "Beverly Hills Is Hit at Realty Convention," *Los Angeles Record*, December 9, 1922.

Chapter 9: Dramatis Personae

1. Eileen Whitfield, *Pickford: The Woman Who Made Hollywood* (Lexington: University Press of Kentucky, 1997).
2. Ibid.
3. Ibid.
4. Mary Pickford, *Sunshine and Shadow* (Garden City, NY: Doubleday & Company, 1955).
5. "Beverly Hills Is Hit at Realty Convention," *Los Angeles Record*, December 9, 1922.
6. Whitfield, *Pickford: The Woman Who Made Hollywood*.
7. Pickford, *Sunshine and Shadow*.

8. Robert S. Birchard, *King Cowboy: Tom Mix and the Movies* (Burbank, CA: Riverwood Press, 1993).

9. Ibid.

10. Richard D. Jensen, *The Amazing Tom Mix: The Most Famous Cowboy of the Movies* (Lincoln, NE: iUniverse, 2005).

11. Gregory Paul Williams, *The Story of Hollywood: An Illustrated History* (Los Angeles: BL Press LLC, 2011).

Chapter 10: Playing with Fire

1. Joan Renner, "How Murderess Clara Phillips Became 'Tiger Girl,'" *Los Angeles Magazine*, June 24, 2013; accessed at LAMag.com., June 24, 2013.

2. Clark Fogg, Senior Forensic Specialist, Beverly Hills Police Department, interview December 15, 2015.

3. "Editor Injured in Bomb Blast: Beverly Hills Publisher Hurt by Infernal Machine; Lays Trouble to Long Dispute," *Los Angeles Examiner*, February 27, 1923.

4. "Beverly Hills Hunts Bomber," *Los Angeles Evening Express*, February 27, 1923.

5. "Hunt Sender of Death Device to Journalist," *Los Angeles Record*, February 28, 1923.

6. "Editor Injured in Bomb Blast: Beverly Hills Publisher Hurt by Infernal Machine; Lays Trouble to Long Dispute," *Los Angeles Examiner*, February 27, 1923.

7. "Beverly Hills Hunts Bomber," *Los Angeles Evening Herald*, February 27, 1923.

8. "Arrest in 24 Hours," *Los Angeles Record*, February 28, 1923.

9. "Reward Posted in 'Bomb' Plot," *Los Angeles Times*, February 28, 1923.

10. "Beverly Hills Hunts Bomber," *Los Angeles Evening Express*, February 27, 1923.

11. "William J. Burns." *Wikipedia: The Free Encyclopedia*. Wikimedia Foundation, Inc., last updated (24 September, 2016); accessed on September 27, 2016 at https://en.wikipedia.org/wiki/William_J._Burns.

12. "Beverly Bomb Sender Sought," *Los Angeles Examiner*, February 28, 1923.

13. Ibid.

14. Email exchange with Michael A. Fratantoni, archivist for the L.A. County Sheriff's Department, dated December 4, 2015.

15. "Bomb Sent Editor as Joke, Is Belief," *Los Angeles Evening Herald*, March 1, 1923.

16. "Bomb Proves to Be Firecrackers," *Los Angeles Record*, March 1, 1923.

17. "'Infernal Machine' Explodes; Firecrackers Injure Editor," *New York Times*, March 1, 1923.

18. B. J. Firminger, "The Story of Beverly Hills," *Beverly Hills Citizen*, May 9, 1941.

19. Minutes of the Board of Trustees of the City of Beverly Hills, March 1, 1923.

20. Minutes of the Board of Trustees of the City of Beverly Hills, March 12, 1923.

21. Resolution #73, City of Beverly Hills, March 12, 1923.

Chapter 11: On Their Own

1. Myrtle Gebhart, "Marry in Haste, and Repent in the Courtroom," *Los Angeles Times*, January 28, 1923.

2. "Plain Water Stirs Beverly," *Los Angeles Examiner*, April 5, 1923.

3. Inspired by a discussion between two characters in Martin Seay, *The Mirror Thief* (Brooklyn, NY: Melville House, 2016).

4. "Sculptor and Actress View Film Memorial," *Los Angeles Times*, July 30, 1959, and "Monument Salutes 8 Annexation Fighters," *Los Angeles Times*, March 15, 1964.

5. Minutes of Meeting, Bureau of Sanitary Engineering, April 7, 1923. Department of Public Health, State Board of Health Records Minutes (February 1923–February 1926) R384.001.

6. "Beverly Water Brings Dispute," *Los Angeles Examiner*, April 21, 1923.

7. Ibid.

8. Ibid.

9. Ibid.

10. Reproduction of the note attached to the water sample, B. J. Firminger, *Beverly Hills Citizen*, May 9, 1941.

11. "Beverly Hills Is Hit at Realty Convention," *Los Angeles Record*, December 9, 1922.

12. "The Weather: Official Report," *Los Angeles Times*, April 24 1923.

13. B. J. Firminger, "The Story of Beverly Hills," *Beverly Hills Citizen*, May 16, 1941.

14. "Beverly Beats Annexation," *Los Angeles Examiner*, April 25, 1923.

15. Section 3, City of Beverly Hills Resolution #73, dated March 12, 1923.

16. "Beverly Beats Annexation," *Los Angeles Examiner*, April 25, 1923.

17. Firminger, "The Story of Beverly Hills," *Beverly Hills Citizen*, May 16, 1941.

18. "Annexation Is Rejected by Beverly," *Los Angeles Times*, April 25, 1923.

19. "Beverly Beats Annexation," *Los Angeles Examiner*, April 25, 1923.

20. Ibid.

21. "Annexation Is Rejected by Beverly," *Los Angeles Times*, April 25, 1923.

22. Pierce E. Benedict and Don Kennedy, *History of Beverly Hills* (Beverly Hills, CA: A. H. Cawston and H. M. Meier, 1934).

23. Firminger, "The Story of Beverly Hills," *Beverly Hills Citizen*, May 16, 1941.

24. Ibid.

25. Benedict and Kennedy, *History of Beverly Hills*.

26. Firminger, "The Story of Beverly Hills," *Beverly Hills Citizen*, May 16, 1941.

27. "Extracts from notes taken from Paul. E. Schwab, September 18, 1962." Courtesy of the Beverly Hills Library Special Collections.

28. Lawrence Quirk, *The Kennedys in Hollywood* (Dallas-Fort Worth, TX: Taylor Publications, 1996).

29. Firminger, "The Story of Beverly Hills," *Beverly Hills Citizen*, May 16, 1941.

Index